T0016131

DEVOTIONS & PRAYERS FOR A

"NO REGRETS" LIFE

"NO REGRETS" LIFE

INSPIRATION & ENCOURAGEMENT FOR TEEN BOYS

PAUL KENT

BARBOUR
PUBLISHING

Published by Barbour Publishing, Inc., 1810 Barbour Drive, Uhrichsville, Ohio 44683, www.barbourbooks.com

Our mission is to inspire the world with the life-changing message of the Bible.

Member of the
Evangelical Christian
Publishers Association

Printed in China.

> **regret** *(noun): sorrow aroused by circumstances beyond one's control or power to repair*

Regret makes you miserable. Who wants to live like that?

The good news is that regret can be avoided. Since you're still young, this is a perfect time to make choices that stop regret before it even starts. And if you already have some regrets (we all do), this is a great time to learn how to deal with them.

Now, let's be clear—in our broken world, *sorrow* is a fact of life. We'll be sad when people we love die or when our own hopes and dreams don't play out. This is absolutely normal.

But there's no need to *add* sorrow to our lives by way of regret. Regret is the ball and chain we drag around due to our own dumb words and actions. "Play stupid games, win stupid prizes," they say—and when we do, we stumble into the minefield of that definition above, those circumstances beyond our control or power to repair.

Yikes.

So let's figure out what creates regret and then walk (preferably, *run*) in the other direction. Let's turn to the ultimate authority, God, learning from His Word what we should and shouldn't do. Let's commit every aspect of our lives to God's Son, Jesus Christ, who breaks the power of sin and tames that horrible beast of regret.

In the following pages, you'll find one hundred practical, Bible-based readings to guide you into a happier, healthier life. Though regret is by definition a negative thing, we're going to keep things fun. We'll highlight some important Dos and Don'ts, always within the bigger picture of God's love and His desire for your well-being.

Nobody wants regret in their lives. Here's your opportunity to put up a big, bold No Trespassing sign. Ready to begin?

1 Imagine yourself fifty years from now. You're in your sixties, close to if not already in your retirement years. You look back over all the decades of your life and say, "Man, I wish I would have played more video games."

Yeah, no.

"Gee, I wish I would have spent more time arguing with my friends and family."

Not that either.

"You know, I wish I would have put way more emphasis on money and things."

Strike three.

The stuff that seems so important in this moment is often the stuff that leads to regret. So let's begin our journey to a no-regrets life with the biggest observation of all:

DO THIS

Live for Something Higher

And not just something, some*one*. You already know who.

No matter what anyone else might say, there is an all-powerful, all-knowing God who created this world and keeps it going day by day. The problems we all face—including our regrets—happen because each and every one of us has rebelled against this incredible Deity:

> *The fool says in his heart, "There is no God." They are corrupt, and their ways are vile; there is no one who does good. God looks down from heaven on all mankind to see if there are any who understand, any who seek God. Everyone has turned away, all have become corrupt; there is no one who does good, not even one.* PSALM 53:1–3 NIV

It's imperative (really, really important) to turn to God, *on His terms.* That's why He gave us His Word, the Bible. It explains who He is and who we are, what He wants and what we should do, where He is and how we can join Him. Step one to a no-regrets life is acknowledging God and our need for the salvation that only Jesus can offer. Never forget:

> *"Salvation is found in no one else, for there is no other name under heaven given to mankind by which we must be saved."*
> ACTS 4:12 NIV

GREAT VERSE TO MEMORIZE!

To know and follow the one true God—the incredible Trinity of Father, Son, and Holy Spirit—is the highest pursuit in this life. It goes far beyond any career or amount of money, any fame or pleasure, even any service you might provide to your fellow man. . .though service to other people will follow as you get serious about God.

If you want to avoid regret, get on the right path—the narrow road that leads to life (Matthew 7:14). Ignore all the distractions along the way. Live for something higher.

I know that the LORD is great, that our Lord is greater than all gods.

PSALM 135:5 NIV

Heavenly Father, so many things fight for my attention, but only You are worthy of my time and energy. Help me to live for higher things—knowing and serving You.

2 Ask a parent or grandparent, and they may tell you the world has gone stark raving mad. Things that were once commonly accepted as good are now somehow "controversial"—maybe even worth a punch in the nose. Beliefs that the vast majority of people held recently, in cultures around the world, will now get you canceled from social media, schools, and jobs.

Having grown up in this environment, you might not recognize the seismic shift in thinking the way older generations do. But as a follower of Jesus, who called Himself "the truth" (John 14:6), you'll want to know and accept reality as it's presented in God's Word, the Bible. You'll protect yourself from regret down the road by holding fast to this rule:

DO THIS

Believe in Truth

Why is that so important? Because believing in truth—agreeing with reality—honors the God who defines reality.

Unless you think the entire universe is some weird illusion, you have to admit that you do exist, in a physical body, in a physical world. Certain rules—like gravity, aging, and death—apply to all people, whether they like it or not. Every person, whatever their background, has some notion of right and wrong. These realities had to have a source, and the Bible offers a compelling explanation:

> *In the beginning God created the heaven and the earth.*
> GENESIS 1:1 SKJV

Many people disagree with the idea of God—and they do it loudly. Granted, the concept of an unexplainable, all-powerful Creator is hard to grasp. But the only real alternative is that the universe somehow created and sustains itself. . .and that takes *way* more faith than believing in God.

If God exists and is who He says, then we are accountable to Him. His rules prevail over our individual wants and wishes. And His desires really aren't mysterious.

> *"I have not spoken in secret, in a dark place of the earth. I did not say to the descendants of Jacob, 'Seek Me in vain.' I, the Lord, speak righteousness. I declare things that are right."*
> ISAIAH 45:19 SKJV

GOD SETS THE STANDARDS!

There is only *one* truth: God's. When He says that "all have sinned and come short" of His glory (Romans 3:23 SKJV), He means it. When He says that "you must be born again" (John 3:7 SKJV), He means it. When He says He is "not willing that any should perish but that all should come to repentance" (2 Peter 3:9 SKJV), He means it.

Believe God's truth, and act on it. You'll never regret that.

> *I will proclaim the name of the Lord; ascribe greatness to our God. He is the Rock. His work is perfect, for all His ways are judgment, a God of truth and without iniquity; just and right is He.*
> DEUTERONOMY 32:3–4 SKJV

Lord, in a world of falsehood, show me Your truth and help me to walk in it.

3 Life is all about choices. And choices are all about trade-offs. Have you ever been irritated with your mom or dad over a decision they made? (Who hasn't?) Maybe they tried to explain how difficult it is—really, *impossible*—to satisfy everyone at the same time. Dad's new job might mean more money but less time with the family. The beach is great for little Lacey, but teenage Tyler likes the amusement park. The youth group with the cool music and light show is weak on Bible teaching. . .and your parents keep looking for a better church.

Something's gotta give, every time. But what ought to give is the lesser choice. To keep yourself on the path to a no-regrets life,

DON'T DO THIS
Jumble Your Priorities

A priority is something that deserves your attention first. For teen guys, schoolwork is a priority over video games. Team practice is a priority over a fast-food run with the guys. Time spent with God—in His Word, in prayer, in self-denial and service to others—is *the* priority over everything else. The Old Testament hero Joshua hammered that home with his fellow Israelites:

> *"If serving the LORD seems undesirable to you, then choose for yourselves this day whom you will serve, whether the gods your ancestors served beyond the Euphrates, or the gods of the Amorites, in whose land you are living. But as for me and my household, we will serve the LORD."* JOSHUA 24:15 NIV

A GREAT "FAREWELL ADDRESS" FROM THE 110-YEAR-OLD JOSHUA

The teen years are a great time to develop good habits for life. You're already reading a devotional—good! But don't just read *about* the Bible. . .*read the Bible*. Make time every day for God's Word and for prayer. Make sure you're attending a Bible-believing, Bible-teaching church as often as you can. Make the effort to say no to your own desires when you know they're not God's desires.

But be careful that you're not just busy. A woman named Martha loved to have Jesus in her home, and she worked like crazy to make everything "just so." Her sister, Mary, on the other hand, just sat and talked with the Lord. Martha stewed, finally barking at Jesus, "Tell her to help me!" (Luke 10:40 NIV).

That is what we call a jumbling of priorities.

> *"Martha, Martha," the Lord answered, "you are worried and upset about many things, but few things are needed—or indeed only one. Mary has chosen what is better, and it will not be taken away from her."* LUKE 10:41–42 NIV

You'll never regret the choice to put Jesus first in your life.

So then, just as you received Christ Jesus as Lord, continue to live your lives in him, rooted and built up in him.
COLOSSIANS 2:6–7 NIV

Jesus, I want to choose the one best thing—my relationship with You. Give me the focus and energy I need to be faithful.

4 You would have liked the Bible character Esther—she was gorgeous. One of perhaps thousands of young women forced into a kind of beauty pageant, Esther captivated King Xerxes, who made her queen.

It's a story of faith and courage, as Esther risked herself to save her fellow Jews. Along the way she received an amazing offer—three times, in fact. "What is your request?" Xerxes asked her. "Even up to half the kingdom, it will be granted" (Esther 7:2; see also 5:3, 6).

Can you imagine getting an offer like that from the most powerful king around? Well, you don't have to imagine it. God has said basically the same thing to you.

To avoid regrets in this life, take full advantage of the offer.

DO THIS

Ask

God made everything, and He retains all rights of ownership: "The earth is the LORD's, and everything in it, the world, and all who live in it" (Psalm 24:1 NIV). To those who follow His Son, God becomes an adoptive Father—a generous one, according to Jesus:

> *"Ask and it will be given to you; seek and you will find; knock and the door will be opened to you. For everyone who asks receives; the one who seeks finds; and to the one who knocks, the door will be opened."* MATTHEW 7:7–8 NIV

EASY-TO-REMEMBER ACRONYM! ASK = ASK, SEEK, KNOCK

Prayer is just talking with God, but sometimes we complicate it. If we've sinned, we feel too dirty to go to Him. If we're worried, we're embarrassed to admit it. If our problem seems small, we can't imagine that God wants to mess with it. But do Jesus' words sound like God would ever ignore your prayers? "Some people think God does not like to be troubled with our constant coming and asking," the famous evangelist D. L. Moody said. "The only way to trouble God is not to come at all."

So ask. If you need help with a class at school, if you want a friend to meet Jesus, if you're looking for a job, if you hope for a date with *that girl*, go straight to God and ask. Then trust Him to give you the right answer.

> *You do not have because you do not ask God. When you ask, you do not receive, because you ask with wrong motives, that you may spend what you get on your pleasures.* James 4:2–3 niv

So. . .there are some limits on the offer, which we'll consider next. But never doubt this: God is a good Father who *wants* to bless you. Don't hesitate to ask.

"If you, then, though you are evil, know how to give good gifts to your children, how much more will your Father in heaven give good gifts to those who ask him!"
Matthew 7:11 niv

Father, I want Your blessing. Here's what's on my heart. . . .

5 Maybe someday you'll be a dad. You'll be responsible for a young life, to provide and protect, to teach and train. To model Christian manhood to a little boy or girl who needs to understand God's intentions for adult life.

You'll want to have fun too. You'll sacrifice time, energy, and money for that little person you love so much, putting up with many inconveniences to make the child's life happier.

But there will be limits. Imagine: Three-year-old Junior crawls into your lap and asks sweetly, "Daddy, can I have an ice cream cone?" *Of course—we're off to the Dairy Delite!* But what if Junior grabs your arm and shouts, "Gimme an ice cream cone!" Things look a bit different, don't they?

Even the heavenly Father balks at some of His kids' "requests." For a no-regrets life, here's an important rule:

DON'T DO THIS
Dictate to God

People are naturally selfish. Even Christians, who have God's Holy Spirit living in them, still wrestle with the "gimmes." We want more money, a new car, a spot on the basketball team, the prettiest girl in school. . .*now*, Lord!

It's not just stuff that we demand. Sometimes we tell God to do things that are, frankly, nuts:

> [Elijah] requested for himself that he might die, and said, "It is enough. Now, O LORD, take away my life, for I am not better than my fathers." 1 KINGS 19:4 SKJV

> But it displeased Jonah exceedingly, and he was very angry. And he prayed to the LORD and said. . ."O LORD, I beseech

You, take my life from me. For it is better for me to die than to live." JONAH 4:1–3 SKJV

Two of God's handpicked prophets dictating to the Lord. . .not a good look.

Jesus shows the way we *should* pray. Here He is in the garden of Gethsemane, the night He would be arrested and sentenced to die on a cross, asking for what He wanted but leaving the matter fully in the Father's hands:

He went a little farther and fell on His face, and prayed, saying, "O My Father, if it is possible, let this cup pass from Me. Nevertheless, not as I will, but as You will." . . . He went away again the second time and prayed, saying, "O My Father, if this cup may not pass away from Me unless I drink it, Your will be done." MATTHEW 26:39, 42 SKJV

NOT EVEN JESUS MADE DEMANDS IN PRAYER.

Fighting God's will always leads to regret. So get on board with Him in your prayers. Ask for what you want, but leave room for Him to answer in His perfect time and way.

"When you pray, say:
Our Father who is in heaven,
Hallowed be Your name.
Your kingdom come.
Your will be done."
LUKE 11:2 SKJV

Lord, my life is all about You. Please bless
me according to Your perfect will.

6 Who are you, really?

It's a simple question, yet it has stumped people for as long as people have existed. The answer would seem to be a combination of our time and place, our natural personality, and our opportunities to learn and grow and achieve.

To answer that question, many men emphasize their accomplishments: "I'm the CEO of a multimillion-dollar company." "I'm an in-demand architect." "I'm a professional bowler." "I'm a Spider-Man impersonator who climbs the walls of New York City skyscrapers." But who we are is a much deeper thing than what we do.

Misunderstandings here can lead to regret, since this question colors our entire lives. Here's an important rule to learn as soon as possible:

DO THIS

Know Your Identity

"How you identify" is a hot topic in our culture. But whatever we claim as our identity needs to align with reality—and reality comes from the God who created all things.

His creation is certainly varied. The physical world includes oceans and deserts, plains and mountains, giant sequoia trees and individual blades of grass. The animal world encompasses everything from ants to blue whales. Our human realm features male and female, tall and short, brilliant and average, "every nation, tribe, people and language" (Revelation 7:9 NIV). But each one of us shares a common identity:

> *For all have sinned and fall short of the glory of God.* ROMANS 3:23 NIV

You may already know that verse. It's the bad news of being human, but it's tucked into some truly excellent news:

> *But now apart from the law the righteousness of God has been made known, to which the Law and the Prophets testify. This righteousness is given through faith in Jesus Christ to all who believe. There is no difference between Jew and Gentile, for all have sinned and fall short of the glory of God, and all are justified freely by his grace through the redemption that came by Christ Jesus. God presented Christ as a sacrifice of atonement, through the shedding of his blood—to be received by faith. He did this to demonstrate his righteousness, because in his forbearance he had left the sins committed beforehand unpunished—he did it to demonstrate his righteousness at the present time, so as to be just and the one who justifies those who have faith in Jesus.* ROMANS 3:21–26 NIV

JUSTIFIED = "MADE RIGHT"

So who are you, really? If you believe in Jesus, you are a much-loved son of God, saved from sin and assured of eternal life. Every choice you make should now be aimed at pleasing the Lord. His Word is your guide, and His grace is your helping hand when you fall. You are completely free to identify *with Him*.

> **Therefore, there is now no condemnation for those who are in Christ Jesus.**
> ROMANS 8:1 NIV

Whatever I pursue as a career, Lord, my true identity is in You. May I reflect You well in this world.

7 "Help me, Obi-Wan Kenobi—you're my only hope."

Millions of *Star Wars* fans recognize this recorded plea of Princess Leia, replayed in hologram form by R2-D2 as Obi-Wan, Luke Skywalker, and C-3PO look on. A rebellion against the evil galactic empire was brewing, and Leia craved the assistance of the man Luke knew only as Ben Kenobi. The youth of Tatooine had no inkling of Ben's history as a Jedi knight and general in the Clone Wars.

In that long-ago, faraway galaxy, Leia's respect for Obi-Wan was well placed—but she was wrong to think he was her *only* hope. Luke Skywalker would play a decisive role in the rebellion, as would a dashing young space pirate named Han Solo.

The modern-day Milky Way is just as troubled as those stars and planets under the galactic empire's control. Like Princess Leia, we have a war to fight, a rebellion against the evil power of Satan. And, like her, we are wise to

DO THIS

Know Where to Find Hope

Too many people put their hope in the wrong things. Money seems powerful, but even a trillion dollars won't automatically save you from cancer. Education and intellectual development are good to a point—but they haven't yet cured cancer. Politicians promise all kinds of good things (including a cure for cancer), but guess what? Politicians fail too, and often.

None of this should be surprising to us. Nor should the actual source of hope:

Paul, an apostle of Christ Jesus by the command of God our Savior and of Christ Jesus our hope. 1 TIMOTHY 1:1 NIV

Consider this devotion a remedial class in basic Christian beliefs. We *know* where our hope lies, but—human as we are—we still often look to the wrong sources. We'll never find true hope in any physical thing, any human achievement, any grand idea, or any person other than our three-in-one God. But when we do acknowledge Him as our hope, we'll be drenched in the stuff:

> *May the God of hope fill you with all joy and peace as you trust in him, so that you may overflow with hope by the power of the Holy Spirit.* ROMANS 15:13 NIV

WE SERVE "THE GOD OF HOPE"!

Today, whatever difficulties and fears you face, consciously place your hope in God alone. You'll come to regret thinking that money or fame or accomplishments or even a girl will carry you through the challenges of this life. The Lord is truly your only hope—and He's just waiting for you to call.

Why, my soul, are you downcast?
Why so disturbed within me?
Put your hope in God, for I will yet praise him,
my Savior and my God.
PSALM 42:5 NIV

Help me, Lord—You're my only hope. I thank You in advance for the strength and protection You'll provide.

8 It was a painful lesson learned before millions of viewers.

In the 2022 SEC football championship in Atlanta, the LSU Tigers started well, keeping the top-ranked Georgia Bulldogs from getting a first down on their opening possession. Then, on offense, LSU moved the ball into field goal range. Unfortunately for the Tigers, the kick was blocked—and even worse, the entire kicking unit seemed to lose focus. They trudged toward the sidelines, ignoring Georgia's Christopher Smith, who grabbed the still-live football and ran it back the other way for a 96-yard touchdown. What might have been an early 3–0 lead for LSU was suddenly a 7–0 deficit. They ultimately lost the game 50–30.

Is there a takeaway for us? Of course:

DON'T DO THIS
Give Up on the Play

If you play baseball, you run hard to first regardless of how you hit the ball. If you're a musician, you keep practicing that piece until you can perform it flawlessly. If you're recovering from an illness or injury, you keep at the rehab until your body is back where you want it to be. You don't give up on the play, whatever "game" you happen to be part of.

To use a biblical term, you *persevere*:

You need to persevere so that when you have done the will of God, you will receive what he has promised. HEBREWS 10:36 NIV

To avoid regret, always stay in the game. When your schoolwork gets harder (and it does, every year), work harder. If you're having problems with family or friends, don't give up on them. If you have a dream for an invention or a business or a ministry of some sort, push through the inevitable reverses you'll experience. You're not guaranteed success, but if you ultimately fail, don't you want to be able to say, "I gave it my very best shot"?

Whatever challenge you face, you'll want to pray about it. And you'll need to persevere even in that:

> "Keep on asking, and you will receive what you ask for. Keep on seeking, and you will find. Keep on knocking, and the door will be opened to you. For everyone who asks, receives. Everyone who seeks, finds. And to everyone who knocks, the door will be opened." MATTHEW 7:7–8 NLT

NOTICE THE REPEATED PHRASE?

Life is hard. To succeed, you need to be tougher—to be totally clear, tougher in the strength that God provides. Look to Him, obey Him, serve Him, and regret won't stand a chance against you.

You do not lack any spiritual gift as you eagerly
wait for our Lord Jesus Christ to be revealed.
He will also keep you firm to the end.
1 CORINTHIANS 1:7–8 NIV

Lord, it's so easy to quit—but I want to push
through to whatever end You have for me.
Give me the perseverance I need.

9 A six-year-old boy was excited to get some money for his birthday. And though his mom and dad urged him to keep the cash in a box in his dresser drawer, Jake chose to carry his loot everywhere he went. "I won't lose it," he insisted—until he lost it.

Before he's ready to make a purchase, a boy is wise to keep his money safe in the old underwear drawer. A teen is wise to park his money in a savings account—or maybe even begin to invest it. If you've ever been given money as a gift or worked hard to earn some, don't let it get away from you. Here's a good rule:

DO THIS

Keep Money in Its Place

If you learn to handle your money wisely now, you'll save yourself a lot of regret as a forty-, fifty-, or sixty-year-old. Working hard, spending less than you earn, and saving for the future are choices that will serve you well through your entire life. And this isn't just some sales pitch from an investment company. . .it's biblical:

> *Dishonest money dwindles away, but whoever gathers money little by little makes it grow.* PROVERBS 13:11 NIV

Of course, the saying "Keep money in its place" has another meaning: don't allow the Benjamins to take over your life. Money is certainly "a thing"—the Bible talks about it a lot—but it can't be "*the* thing." Have you heard what the apostle Paul told his young friend and helper Timothy?

> *Those who want to get rich fall into temptation and a trap and into many foolish and harmful desires that plunge people into ruin and destruction. For the love of money is a root of all kinds of evil. Some people, eager for money, have wandered*

from the faith and pierced themselves with many griefs.
1 Timothy 6:9–10 niv

MONEY ITSELF ISN'T EVIL—BUT THE LOVE OF MONEY SURE IS TROUBLE.

This world certainly loves money and thinks you should too. But you don't have to look hard to see the "foolish and harmful desires that plunge people into ruin." For a no-regrets life, be different. Don't be like the actors and athletes, the musicians and influencers who think life is all about CA$H. Let Paul finish his thought: "But you, man of God, flee from all this, and pursue righteousness, godliness, faith, love, endurance and gentleness" (1 Timothy 6:11 niv).

When you commit yourself to Jesus, God commits to taking care of you. And He provides far more than simple money ever could.

"Everyone who has left houses or brothers or sisters or father or mother or wife or children or fields for my sake will receive a hundred times as much and will inherit eternal life."

Matthew 19:29 niv

Heavenly Father, I need money in this life—but I need You more. Please give me the resources I need to live on, but don't ever let me be consumed by them.

10 When you really like a girl, you want to know everything about her. Maybe you've felt that way. If not, it'll sneak up on you someday.

We're not discussing some passing thought like *Hmm, Katie's kind of cute*—we mean the time when you're totally wrecked by *"This girl!"* She's all you can think about, and you want to know more, *more*, MORE: where she comes from, what she likes, how she spends her time, who else she's thinking of—well, no, you don't want to go there.

Our love for God is certainly different than those breathless romantic feelings we get from time to time. But the desire to know more about Him should be similar. One of God's wonderful and mysterious characteristics is that He is three "persons" in one—and to really know Him, we need to

DO THIS

Understand the Trinity

Now, nobody can totally understand how God the Father, Jesus the Son, and the Holy Spirit are each distinct persons and yet one God. Good news: He's gracious, so even if we honestly struggle with such things, He still loves us. But we'll regret not digging deeper into this amazing, three-in-one Lord "Who carries our heavy loads day by day. . .the God Who saves us" (Psalm 68:19 NLV).

Here is Jesus describing the Trinity's work:

> *"The Helper is the Holy Spirit. The Father will send Him in My place. He will teach you everything and help you remember everything I have told you."* JOHN 14:26 NLV

THE WORD *TRINITY* ISN'T IN THE BIBLE—BUT THE IDEA SURE IS.

God the Father—like any good dad—is the driving force in the family. But He's incredibly fond of His perfect Son, Jesus, through whom He made the universe and who will ultimately restore and rule it. By His Spirit, God lives in every person who follows Jesus by faith. The Trinity's work is to make you like Jesus, benefiting you forever and bringing honor and glory to God.

One of Jesus' closest friends on earth, the apostle Peter, wrote,

> *You were chosen by God the Father long ago. He knew you were to become His children. You were set apart for holy living by the Holy Spirit. May you obey Jesus Christ and be made clean by His blood.* 1 PETER 1:2 NLV

Father, Son, and Spirit are all eternal, all equal, and all one. Yeah, it's a mystery that has stumped human beings for millennia. But it's a mystery that's totally worth your time and attention today.

May you have loving-favor from our Lord Jesus Christ. May you have the love of God. May you be joined together by the Holy Spirit.
2 CORINTHIANS 13:14 NLV

I don't get it, Lord—but I don't have to understand the Trinity to believe it. . .to believe You. Please give me the desire and ability to know You better.

11 You're aware of false advertising, right? Companies often promote their products in misleading ways. They might photoshop pictures or highlight a price without hidden fees or make exaggerated claims that catch your attention but turn out to be untrue.

Nobody can accuse God of false advertising.

He says His "product"—a relationship with Him now and eternal life to follow—is incredible, and He's absolutely right. But God is also up front about the costs. No, you don't have to pay for salvation—that's a free gift of His grace through faith in Jesus (Romans 5:15–18). But contrary to what some misinformed people say, your Christian life will not be easy. You will "pay" when you seriously follow the Lord.

It's important to understand this so you're not tempted to bail out when things get tough.

DON'T DO THIS
Be Surprised by the Struggle

The Bible's promises of strength, protection, peace, and joy are being fulfilled in your life now. But they will be *completely* experienced in eternity. Right now, God is helping you through the hardships of a broken world, where accidents, diseases, relationship problems, and strong temptations can make you half-crazy. Some of our struggles are against this sin-cursed earth; many come from people who hate our faith:

> *Yes, and all who will live godly in Christ Jesus shall suffer persecution. But evil men and seducers shall become worse and worse.* 2 TIMOTHY 3:12–13 SKJV

We wonder why things are so hard—but God is using our struggles to draw us closer to Jesus:

Beloved, do not think it strange concerning the fiery trial that is to try you as though some strange thing happened to you. But rejoice because you are partakers of Christ's sufferings, that when His glory shall be revealed you may be glad also with exceeding joy. If you are reproached for the name of Christ, happy are you, for the Spirit of glory and of God rests on you. On their part, He is slandered, but on your part, He is glorified. But let none of you suffer as a murderer, or as a thief, or as an evildoer, or as a busybody in other men's matters. Yet if any man suffers as a Christian, let him not be ashamed, but let him glorify God in this matter.
1 PETER 4:12–16 SKJV

BE THANKFUL FOR HOW MANY THINGS GO *RIGHT* IN LIFE!

Reread that last phrase: "Let him glorify God in this matter." Ultimately, that's your purpose in life. Chasing ease and pleasure leads to regret. But by glorifying God, you'll get to enjoy every good thing He has advertised.

"I have spoken these things to you, that in Me you might have peace. In the world you shall have tribulation, but be of good cheer: I have overcome the world."
JOHN 16:33 SKJV

Lord, keep me faithful through the struggles of this life. I know You'll reward me completely in heaven.

12 It may be hard to believe, but at one time—not so long ago—there were far fewer information options. Most cities had one or two newspapers and a television station for each of the three major networks. Families generally owned a single telephone (connected to the wall by a cord), and "texting" took place through the mail. Back then, it was called "writing letters."

Now you carry the world in the palm of your hand. Millions of websites bring you news, sports, politics, culture. . .information of every imaginable kind. Questions that once took weeks to answer now take milliseconds. The world is immensely better for all this.

Or maybe not.

Technology often outpaces wisdom. We are drowning in data but dry in discernment. We really need help to analyze all the information available to us. Here's a good rule to remember:

DO THIS

Make God's Word Your Fact-Checker

God provided the Bible to help us understand life. Where did we come from? Where are we going? Why is there so much pain in the world? (And, relatedly, *Why are people so crazy?*) What is this life really all about? God's Word has the answers to these questions—and thousands of others besides.

The better we know the Bible, the better our lives will be. And the better our lives are, the fewer regrets we'll have:

> *All scripture is given by inspiration of God and is profitable for doctrine, for reproof, for correction, for instruction in righteousness, that the man of God may be perfect, thoroughly furnished for all good works.* 2 TIMOTHY 3:16 SKJV

ONE TRUTH, NEVER CHANGING

Millions of voices scream for your attention, but God's is the only one that matters. And though He does sometimes thunder (2 Samuel 22:14), more often God speaks quietly, like He did to the prophet Elijah:

> *Behold, the LORD passed by, and a great and strong wind tore the mountains and broke the rocks in pieces before the LORD, but the LORD was not in the wind. And after the wind there was an earthquake, but the LORD was not in the earthquake. And after the earthquake there was a fire, but the LORD was not in the fire. And after the fire a still small voice.* 1 KINGS 19:11–12 SKJV

You'll "hear" God's voice as you read and study the Bible. He'll talk to you through His Spirit, in words that align perfectly with the written Word that does not change.

Screen everything you hear—from the media, friends, teachers, even your church—through the filter of God's Word. When your thoughts and actions are truly biblical, you'll keep regrets at a safe distance.

Your word is a lamp to my feet and a light to my path.
PSALM 119:105 SKJV

Lord, Your opinion is the only one that matters. Please help me to know Your mind through Your Word.

13 Sure, some of the choices we make are more consequential than others. But every decision, no matter how small, matters.

For example, does it really hurt anything if you choose a cream-filled donut instead of fresh fruit for breakfast? You're young and active, and your body can burn off the fat and calories, right? Probably. But if the cream-filled donut option becomes your breakfast default, the fat and calories will ultimately catch up to you. And if you make similar choices for your lunch and supper, you'll definitely regret it over time. Your weight, your blood pressure, and your overall health and well-being will suffer when you eat the wrong things consistently.

In your diet—and in any number of other important issues in life—here's a great rule of thumb:

DO THIS

Take the Long View

Teen guys tend to live in the moment. What do I want to eat *right now*? Where do I want to go *right now*? How am I going to feel happier *right now*? (Actually, a lot of people of all ages think like that—but hey, this is a book for teen guys.)

The choice to feel good right now, though, isn't always the best one. The moment may offer food or sex or spending or medication or sleeping in or staying up late—all appropriate things in their appropriate times and places. . .but potentially troublesome otherwise. So take the long view, considering what today's pleasures might mean to the twenty-, thirty-, or forty-year-old you.

By faith Moses, when he had grown up, refused to be known as the son of Pharaoh's daughter. He chose to be mistreated along with the people of God rather than to enjoy the fleeting pleasures of sin. HEBREWS 11:24–25 NIV

Maybe you suddenly feel like a courtroom lawyer on TV. You're ready to argue, "Objection! The record shows that Moses' decision brought him mistreatment. Therefore it was a poor choice!"

But Moses experienced and accomplished great things in life because he looked ahead. His choices weren't based on his immediate feelings. Yes, he went through hardship, but the hardship led to the best possible outcome for his life—a deep and lasting relationship with God.

The LORD would speak to Moses face to face, as one speaks to a friend. EXODUS 33:11 NIV

NOW, *THERE'S* A LIFE GOAL.

And isn't that the longest view of all—the eternal life you're given through faith in Jesus? Though you may not sense it yet, this life is flying by. Keep an eye on that longer, better life God has planned for you.

You make known to me the path of life; you will fill me with joy in your presence, with eternal pleasures at your right hand.
PSALM 16:11 NIV

Give me the long view, Lord, both of this life and of the life to come. I want to spend my time wisely.

14 In a perfect world, parents love each other and their kids. Everyone sticks together, the family unit is productive, and good feelings surround everyone like a soft, warm blanket.

Unfortunately, we don't live in a perfect world.

Hopefully, you're part of an excellent family. But we all know that many guys grow up in less than ideal circumstances. Wherever you fall on the happy home scale, beware of a dangerous medical condition known as CTGS: Crabby Teenage Guy Syndrome. (Okay, I made that up.) But crabby teenage guys are real. Isn't it true that *you*—like every other teen guy in the world, all through history— occasionally create tension and drama in your home?

For a no-regrets life, here's an important rule:

DON'T DO THIS

Disrespect Your Parents

If you've been around God's people for any amount of time, you've probably heard the fifth of the Ten Commandments: "Honor your father and mother" (Exodus 20:12 NLT). That rule is repeated word for word in Deuteronomy 5:16, Matthew 15:4, Mark 7:10, Luke 18:20, and Ephesians 6:2—and the general idea appears in many other passages. Check out this little commentary from a guy named Agur:

> *The eye that mocks a father and despises a mother's instructions will be plucked out by ravens of the valley and eaten by vultures.* PROVERBS 30:17 NLT

YEAH, THE BIBLE REALLY SAYS THAT.

By creating Eve to be Adam's wife, God set up marriage as the first great human institution. And when marriage leads to children,

God's plan is for kids to respect, obey, and learn from their parents. That creates a stable structure for all of society, a pattern that— when followed—allows unrelated and dissimilar people to live successfully side by side.

This idea is so important that God actually threatened *death* on rebellious Old Testament kids:

> *"Suppose a man has a stubborn and rebellious son who will not obey his father or mother, even though they discipline him. In such a case, the father and mother must take the son to the elders as they hold court at the town gate. . . . Then all the men of his town must stone him to death. In this way, you will purge this evil from among you, and all Israel will hear about it and be afraid."* DEUTERONOMY 21:18–19, 21 NLT

You're not that stubborn, right? But that's all the more reason for you to treat Mom or Dad respectfully, every time. No parent is perfect. But all parents—in some form or fashion—want good for their kids. Work with them. You'll never regret showing your parents honor.

Children, always obey your parents, for this pleases the Lord.
COLOSSIANS 3:20 NLT

Heavenly Father, I want a happy home. Help me to respect my parents, and cause us all to grow to be more like Jesus.

15 Every generation has its political scandals. In your grandparents' time, it was Watergate.

The name belonged to a Washington, DC, office complex, where the headquarters of the Democratic National Committee was burglarized in the summer of 1972. Supporters of President Richard Nixon were implicated, and a snowballing scandal led to his resignation two years later.

Several Nixon aides spent time in prison, including his top lawyer and feared "hatchet man," Chuck Colson. Before serving his time, though, Colson found Jesus. Skeptics speculated that he was angling for a lesser sentence—but the final forty years of Colson's life proved that his conversion was absolutely real.

God can and does save unlikely people. As members of His family, we are wise to treat others like He does:

DO THIS

Show Grace

The fact is that every one of us needed (and still needs) God's grace. He is kind to those of us who have chosen to follow Him, to those who are considering His claims on their lives, and to those who oppose Him at every turn. Jesus taught,

> "I say, love your enemies! Pray for those who persecute you! In that way, you will be acting as true children of your Father in heaven. For he gives his sunlight to both the evil and the good, and he sends rain on the just and the unjust alike."
> MATTHEW 5:44–45 NLT

Don't invite regret into your life by being harsh with people who could one day be your spiritual brothers and sisters. And don't even be harsh with yourself whenever you're tempted and give in to sin. Yes, God hates sin—but He loves everyone who believes in His Son, Jesus Christ. God understands that on this earth we will struggle—and He planned to show us grace when we simply admit our failures to Him.

> *If we confess our sins to him, he is faithful and just to forgive us our sins and to cleanse us from all wickedness.* 1 JOHN 1:9 NLT

IT'S SIMPLE, IF NOT ALWAYS EASY—YOU JUST HAVE TO HUMBLE YOURSELF.

God's immense justice is balanced by His incredible grace. . .and it all centers on the death, burial, and resurrection of Jesus. When you honestly, humbly believe in Jesus' sacrifice for your sin, God is happy to show you His grace. Now go and do the same to others.

> *"My life is worth nothing to me unless I use it for finishing the work assigned me by the Lord Jesus—the work of telling others the Good News about the wonderful grace of God."*
> ACTS 20:24 NLT

Sometimes it's hard to show grace, Lord—people can be so rude and selfish and seemingly unworthy of my kindness. But I was all of those things too, and You still welcomed me into Your family. Please help me show grace to everyone I meet.

16 The previous reading encouraged you to show grace to yourself and others. God is gracious (He shows compassion and mercy to troubled people), so follow His example—even when the troubled person is *you.*

When you sin, admit it to God immediately and then move on. Don't beat yourself up over something He's forgiven—remember, He promises in 1 John 1:9 to completely forgive the sins you confess. Don't fret over failure, because God knows it happens. (Why else would we even *have* 1 John 1:9?) Don't ignore Jesus' work on the cross by thinking you are somehow responsible for your own salvation. You're not.

Grace is a beautiful thing. But it only applies to those who truly, humbly want to obey God—it's never a license for sin. To keep yourself on the path to a no-regrets life, here's an important rule:

DON'T DO THIS
Give Yourself a Pass

How does that differ from showing yourself grace? Grace is for moments of weakness when you do something you know is wrong. You confess it to God as sin, because you agree with His standards in His Word.

In contrast, when you give yourself a pass, you're saying your thoughts or actions *aren't* wrong. Sure, the Bible might say that greed or lust or stealing or hatred is sin, but "I don't really think so." For the counterargument (not this author's, but God's), see the verses leading up to 1 John 1:9:

> *God is light; in him there is no darkness at all. If we claim to have fellowship with him and yet walk in the darkness, we lie and do not live out the truth. But if we walk in the light, as he*

> *is in the light, we have fellowship with one another, and the blood of Jesus, his Son, purifies us from all sin. If we claim to be without sin, we deceive ourselves and the truth is not in us.* 1 JOHN 1:5–8 NIV

We can't say we have never sinned, and we shouldn't say that our ungodly behaviors are anything but sinful. Giving yourself a pass, spiritually speaking, will lead to serious regret. Instead, do everything in your power to deny your feelings, control your body, and follow the apostle Paul's example:

> *One thing I do: Forgetting what is behind and straining toward what is ahead, I press on toward the goal to win the prize for which God has called me heavenward in Christ Jesus.* PHILIPPIANS 3:13–14 NIV

HERE'S A GREAT "LIFE VERSE"!

There's no coasting in the Christian life. Accept grace when you stumble, but otherwise run as hard as you can toward God.

Do you not know that in a race all the runners run, but only one gets the prize? Run in such a way as to get the prize.
1 CORINTHIANS 9:24 NIV

It's so easy to go easy on myself, Lord.
Discipline me to press on toward holiness.

17 Would you like to have a dollar for every time your parents told you "no"?

"Can I have ice cream for breakfast?"

No.

"Can I play with these matches?"

No.

"Can I watch *Killer Zombie Chainsaw Party*?"

No.

All this negativity, you see, was really positive. Your parents were training you, steering you clear of things that are harmful. Now, as a teenager, you're taking more responsibility for your own choices, and telling yourself "no" sometimes (even *often*) is a great way to hold off regret down the road.

DO THIS

Deny Yourself

This world will push you to do whatever you feel. Your own emotions will do the same. Push back. Say no to the voice in your head that tells you to be lazy, to overeat, to rush into sex, to cheat your employer, to drink or take drugs, to twist the hard truths of the Bible into something easier and "nicer." Deny yourself the immediate, feel-good choice. When you do, things go better for you and the people you care about.

> Then Jesus said to His disciples, "If any man wants to come after Me, let him deny himself, and take up his cross, and follow Me. For whoever will save his life shall lose it, and whoever will lose his life for My sake shall find it." MATTHEW 16:24–25 SKJV

THINK ABOUT THIS: JESUS TOOK UP HIS CROSS FOR *OTHER* PEOPLE, NOT HIMSELF.

God has great plans for your life. Satan is trying hard to stuff those plans in the shredder, douse them with gasoline, and blast them with a flamethrower. He's strong and smart, but God is far more so—and God will help you say no to your own unhealthy desires if you ask.

Now, let's be clear: nobody says that this will be easy.

> *In your struggle against sin, you have not yet resisted to the point of shedding your blood.* HEBREWS 12:4 NIV

"Easy" doesn't accomplish great things. It wasn't easy for Jesus to die on the cross for your sins. But since He did, why not show your gratitude by doing hard things in His honor? Deny yourself, today and every day. You won't regret it.

For the grace of God that brings salvation has appeared to all men, teaching us that, denying ungodliness and worldly lusts, we should live soberly, righteously, and godly in this present world, looking for that blessed hope and the glorious appearing of the great God and our Savior Jesus Christ.
TITUS 2:11–13 SKJV

I am pulled in so many directions, Lord, by this world and by my own emotions. Give me the strength to say no to sin, to deny myself the pleasures that will create regret.

18 Here's an interesting little Bible study: check out all the people to whom Jesus said, "Follow Me."

There were the future apostles Peter and Andrew, who were fishing for a living (Matthew 4:18–20); Matthew, who was collecting taxes for Rome (Matthew 9:9); and Philip, who was probably a follower of John the Baptist at the time (John 1:29–43).

And there were others, including a rich young man who couldn't give up his possessions (Matthew 19:16–22); Peter, again, after he had denied knowing Jesus (John 21:15–22); and anyone who wants to be Jesus' disciple (Mark 8:34).

Following Jesus is the best possible choice you can make in this life. What's the worst? That's answered by the following rule for a no-regrets life:

DON'T DO THIS

Follow Your Heart

"Follow your heart" is a favorite theme of books and movies for kids. As the storyline goes, adults—many times, your parents—are holding you back. To be truly happy, you need to break away from their expectations and do what you love, be who you are. You need to follow your heart!

Sounds good, right? Well, before *you* run off to do your own thing, consider this warning from the Bible:

> The heart is deceitful above all things and beyond cure. Who can understand it? JEREMIAH 17:9 NIV

Our hearts can and will steer us wrong. No, not the muscle that's thumping in your chest right now—we're talking about the desires and emotions and will that make you who you are. God created "the heart" in His own image, to have a relationship with Him. But sin has warped the human heart, which is now a totally unreliable guide to anything good.

Jesus described the human heart in action:

> *"What comes out of a person is what defiles them. For it is from within, out of a person's heart, that evil thoughts come—sexual immorality, theft, murder, adultery, greed, malice, deceit, lewdness, envy, slander, arrogance and folly. All these evils come from inside and defile a person."* MARK 7:20–23 NIV

NOBODY HAD TO TEACH US TO DO WRONG. . .RIGHT?

When you choose to follow Jesus, He sends His Spirit into your heart to counteract the selfish and sinful desires that define the unsaved person. But as long as we live on this earth, we'll battle our "old self," as the apostle Paul called it (Ephesians 4:22 NIV; you can read about his own struggles in Romans 7). To avoid regrets in this life, don't follow your heart—fight it.

See to it, brothers and sisters, that none of you has a sinful, unbelieving heart that turns away from the living God.
HEBREWS 3:12 NIV

Lord, my heart wants all kinds of things that go against Your Word. I need Your help to do what's right. I thank You in advance for the strength You'll give me.

19 "My comments were taken out of context" is a common defense for politicians. They mean there's more to the story than just the apparently dumb statement their opponents have latched on to. A five-second sound bite sometimes does need the larger context of a whole five-minute interview to be properly understood. (Though at times even the context doesn't help—politicians just say some dumb things.)

The Bible *never* says dumb things—though some people want to make it seem that way. While the overall message of God's love for people is simple, it's found in a very large book that can be confusing at times. That's especially true when we see only bits and snatches of scripture.

Here's an important rule for approaching God's Word:

DO THIS

Read Bible Verses in Context

The Merriam-Webster Online Dictionary defines *context* as "the parts of a discourse that surround a word or passage and can throw light on its meaning." I'll warn you right now that the following quotation from scripture—though totally accurate—also totally lacks context:

> *"Unless you are circumcised as required by the law of Moses, you cannot be saved."* Acts 15:1 NLT

A little background: Circumcision is a minor surgery God commanded the ancient Jews to perform when a baby boy was eight days old. (Look it up if you need to.) It set the Jews apart from other nations, identifying them as God's people. This law was a big deal in Old Testament times. . .but has nothing to do with faith in Jesus. People are saved simply by believing in Him, not by any ceremonial actions.

The missing context of the verse above is this: those words were spoken by traditional Jews who thought "the Gentile converts must be circumcised and required to follow the law of Moses" (verse 5 NLT). The rest of Acts 15 shows that the early Christian leaders—all Jewish men themselves—rejected that argument. As Peter said, "We should not make it difficult for the Gentiles who are turning to God" (verse 19 NLT).

The apostle Paul, who was part of that conversation, later scolded Christians in Galatia for disregarding the truth they'd been taught:

> *I am shocked that you are turning away so soon from God, who called you to himself through the loving mercy of Christ. You are following a different way that pretends to be the Good News but is not the Good News at all. You are being fooled by those who deliberately twist the truth concerning Christ.* GALATIANS 1:6–7 NLT

PAUL CALLED THEM "FOOLISH GALATIANS" IN 3:1!

The Galatians missed the full context of Paul's teaching. Let's be sure we never do that ourselves. Messing up Bible truth will definitely lead to regret.

I rejoice in your word like one who discovers a great treasure.
PSALM 119:162 NLT

Thank You for Your Word, Lord—now please help me to read it carefully, in context, with an eye toward obeying it.

20 You see some crazy thing online about someone you don't particularly like—a politician, an athlete or entertainer, even a classmate. Of course, *everyone* needs to know how dumb that person is, right?

Wrong. Majorly wrong.

In a world that's already smoldering with insecurities, resentment, and hatred, why add fuel to the fire? Here's a rule that will save you and others a lot of regret over time:

DON'T DO THIS

Like, Forward, or Otherwise Share Junk

There are countless reasons to handle social media with care. For one thing, you don't know if much of the stuff crossing your screen is actually true. And even if it is true, do you really want to hurt someone by sharing it? Would you enjoy being on the receiving end of that juicy tidbit you're about to send out? How are you going to look tomorrow, next week, or next year if your name is all over some mean-spirited online spat? Social media, as they say, is forever.

The apostle Paul knew more about prison cells than cell phones. But his advice to Christians applies just as well in our twenty-first century as it did in his first:

> *Get rid of all bitterness, rage and anger, brawling and slander, along with every form of malice. Be kind and compassionate to one another, forgiving each other, just as in Christ God forgave you.* EPHESIANS 4:31–32 NIV

SHARE *THIS!*

Notice your responsibility in these verses. *You* need to "get rid of" the angry, malicious feelings that lead to social media skirmishes.

You should be kind and compassionate and forgiving. You don't do these things to earn salvation, which is totally God's gift through your faith in Jesus. But once you're in "the family," you have a responsibility—and it's not sniping at people online.

God has bigger and better things for His kids than down-in-the-mud squabbles on social media. Resist the impulse to insult today, and you'll look back tomorrow without regret. One of the Bible's "wisdom books," Proverbs, boils it all down like this:

> *Whoever. . .spreads slander is a fool. Sin is not ended by multiplying words, but the prudent hold their tongues.* PROVERBS 10:18–19 NIV

The more we talk (or, in this case, type), the greater the danger of saying something stupid—something we'll wish we'd never said. If you have trouble controlling your words, ask God for help. He'll be happy to answer that prayer.

Do not repay evil with evil or insult with insult. On the contrary, repay evil with blessing, because to this you were called so that you may inherit a blessing. For, "Whoever would love life and see good days must keep their tongue from evil and their lips from deceitful speech."
1 PETER 3:9–10 NIV

Lord, please guide my lips—and my fingers— to express words of kindness and healing.

21 PJ, a scrawny seventh grader, joined the track team. He wasn't particularly athletic, but hey—pretty much anyone can run, right?

He preferred the short sprints. PJ was always gasping for breath at the end, but at least they were done in a matter of seconds. The distance runners were chugging around the track for five or six, ten or twelve minutes. That sounded like torture.

In his races, though, PJ almost invariably placed fourth. Only the top three finishers scored points for their team.

One day, when both the junior and senior high teams were practicing at the track, a popular, good-looking twelfth grader—a distance runner—pulled PJ aside. "You know, you're really built for distance," the older guy said. "You ought to work yourself up to the longer races." PJ said, "Hmm, yeah, maybe," but thought to himself, *Who are you to tell me what to do?*

Guess what? PJ looks back on that moment with regret. And he would tell you,

DO THIS
Listen to Advice

Of course, you're not going to do everything everybody tells you (more on that in the next reading). But if someone is willing to reach out and offer insight for your life, at least make an effort to hear what they're saying. In many cases, their speaking up shows love.

Advice—also known as "counsel"—is something God has written into His script for this human movie we're all part of:

> *The way of fools seems right to them, but the wise listen to advice.* PROVERBS 12:15 NIV

Where there is strife, there is pride, but wisdom is found in those who take advice. Proverbs 13:10 NIV

Plans fail for lack of counsel, but with many advisers they succeed. Proverbs 15:22 NIV

Your parents, your pastor, your teachers and coaches, older people in the neighborhood—they've all lived longer than you and learned a lot of things you have yet to grasp. So when they speak, listen. As the very good man Job said,

"Is not wisdom found among the aged? Does not long life bring understanding?" Job 12:12 NIV

WHO DO YOU KNOW WITH GREAT UNDERSTANDING?

To be sure, there are both wise and foolish people of all ages—so whatever advice is offered, listen carefully and then check it out against God's Word. If it stacks up, give it some additional thought. Good counsel can truly change your life, so never dismiss it out of hand.

The heart of the discerning acquires knowledge,
for the ears of the wise seek it out.
Proverbs 18:15 NIV

Lord God, don't let pride keep me from hearing
good advice. I want to be open to Your leading
through the wise people You've put in my life.

22 We just said you should *listen* to advice. Especially if the person offering it (a) knows and loves you, (b) is older and more experienced than you, and (c) is a committed follower of Jesus. People who don't meet every qualification can still offer good insights, but treat their thoughts like a big-screen TV box that says HANDLE WITH CARE.

Because some advice is—how can we say this delicately?—dumb.

Regrets happen when we follow the wrong people and their wrong ideas. So here's a very important rule for life:

DON'T DO THIS
Take All Advice

The Old Testament shares a fascinating story about a guy taking bad advice: Rehoboam, the son of Solomon. You may already know that Solomon was called the wisest king ever. But he got off track with God and did some incredibly foolish things. Rehoboam, next in line for the throne, sadly chose to imitate his dad's bad side.

Solomon ruled over Israel's "golden age," a time of peace and prosperity made possible by the good leadership of his father, David. Solomon built God's temple in Jerusalem as well as a whole lot of other things—but over a forty-year reign imposed heavy taxes and forced labor on his people.

When Solomon died, the Israelites asked Rehoboam to relax Solomon's burdens. He spoke first to some older government officials who encouraged him to be gentle with the people. But Rehoboam ultimately took the advice of his peers:

The young men who had grown up with him replied, "These people have said to you, 'Your father put a heavy yoke on us,

> *but make our yoke lighter.' Now tell them, 'My little finger is thicker than my father's waist. My father laid on you a heavy yoke; I will make it even heavier. My father scourged you with whips; I will scourge you with scorpions.' "* 1 KINGS 12:10–11 NIV

AGGRESSIVE, BOASTFUL TALK IS NEVER THE GODLY WAY.

Dumb advice, even dumber to take it—and the people, understandably offended by Rehoboam's response, broke away to begin their own nation. (This is when Israel divided into two rival nations: one still called Israel to the north, and Judah to the south, where Rehoboam ruled over only two of twelve tribes.)

At one point, the new king even had to run for his life from angry Israelites. He had touched off a kind of civil war that simmered for centuries (2 Chronicles 10:17–19).

Following bad counsel changed everything for Rehoboam and the people under his care. Pray that you never take equally poor advice.

Wisdom will save you from the ways of wicked men, from men whose words are perverse, who have left the straight paths to walk in dark ways.
PROVERBS 2:12–13 NIV

There are so many people who have ideas for me, Lord—but I want to follow only Your wise counsel. Give me the wisdom I need to judge well.

23 Your school classes are supposed to teach you more than just algebra or biology or English composition. All of those homework assignments and writing projects—ideally—help you learn to schedule your time, focus your energies, and see a project through to completion. These are all important skills for adult life.

But a lot of guys (maybe all of us?) are slow to see the value of this process. We'd rather play video games, watch TV or YouTube, sleep in, chill out. . .pretty much anything other than dive into those assignments. It may feel good at first—but the regrets come when you have to pull an all-nighter to finish a paper or you start failing exams because you just never got around to studying.

Today's rule for a no-regrets life is simple:

DO THIS

Work First, Relax Later

Your mom or dad probably works a lot—at an office, in a store, on a construction site, wherever. And when they're home they're probably cooking or cleaning or managing other chores, in addition to volunteering at church or with your school or in the community. They learned their lessons of time management when they were young, and now they're setting an example for you.

That example is a biblical one. Relaxation should come only *after* the work is done:

> I went past the field of a sluggard, past the vineyard of someone who has no sense; thorns had come up everywhere, the ground was covered with weeds, and the stone wall was in ruins. I applied my heart to what I observed and learned a lesson from what I saw: A little sleep, a little slumber, a little folding of the hands to rest—and poverty will come on you like

Too much chillin', and things fall apart. . .sometimes literally.

Through laziness, the rafters sag; because of idle hands, the house leaks. ECCLESIASTES 10:18 NIV

GREAT WORD PICTURE, HUH?

You probably don't own a house yet, but maybe you have a car. This verse could say, "Through laziness, the oil drips out; because of idle hands, the engine seizes up." Or, if you have a pet, "Through laziness, Luna goes hungry; because of idle hands, Luna starves to death."

Whew. . .

Growing up means we learn priorities and act on that knowledge. Yes, it takes work—but working first often saves you effort in the long run. And there's no regret in that.

We do not want you to become lazy, but to imitate those who through faith and patience inherit what has been promised.
HEBREWS 6:12 NIV

I know I need rest, Lord, but I also need to learn to work. Help me do my jobs first then enjoy my relaxation time without any guilt.

24 Movies are an escape from reality. For a couple of hours, you can visit a faraway planet or fly through the sky with a superhero or watch a team of lovable losers win it all. But never look to Hollywood for actual fact.

Even biopics and based-on-a-true-story dramas contain plenty of fiction. And if you're looking for anything related to the Bible or Christian living, you're wise to be very skeptical of what you see on-screen.

That's certainly true of Hollywood's treatment of Satan. Movies and TV shows usually make him totally creepy or comically silly. But the Bible presents Satan as God's sworn enemy who "masquerades as an angel of light" (2 Corinthians 11:14 NIV). We'll avoid his destructive lies—and a whole lot of regret—if we

DO THIS

Understand the Devil

Satan is real. He is God's enemy, though not God's equal—the devil was created, just like we are. He's a fallen angel who wanted to take God's place. For His own purposes, God has given Satan the freedom to harass people since the very beginning.

It was the devil, in the form of a serpent, who got Adam and Eve to disobey God's one rule in the garden of Eden. That "original sin" explains all the pain and frustration and downright tragedy we experience. And Satan is still doing all he can to keep people from God:

> *I am afraid that just as Eve was deceived by the serpent's cunning, your minds may somehow be led astray from your sincere and pure devotion to Christ.* 2 CORINTHIANS 11:3 NIV

If the devil can keep you from believing in Jesus, he wins you for all eternity. But even as a committed Christian, you'll face Satan's temptations and trials. That's why it's so important to study your Bible, pray, and have good Christian friendships. The more defenses you have, the better you'll be able to resist:

> *Put on the full armor of God, so that you can take your stand against the devil's schemes.* EPHESIANS 6:11 NIV

THE APOSTLE PAUL ALSO SAID,
"WE ARE NOT UNAWARE OF HIS SCHEMES" (2 CORINTHIANS 2:11 NIV).

Corrie ten Boom was a Dutch woman who hid Jews from the Nazis during World War II. (If you don't know her story, *The Hiding Place* is definitely worth a read.) She wrote, "It is foolish to underestimate the power of Satan, but it is fatal to overestimate it." What she meant is this: Satan *is* dangerous, much more powerful than we are in our own strength. But Satan is absolutely inferior to God, as Job 1–2 proves. Don't live in fear. Fight in God's strength. You can't lose.

Be alert and of sober mind. Your enemy the devil
prowls around like a roaring lion looking for someone
to devour. Resist him, standing firm in the faith.
1 PETER 5:8–9 NIV

Lord God, keep me close to You so Satan can't squeeze
into my life. Protect me from his lies with Your truth.

25 You've probably heard the phrase "survival of the fittest." It has a specific meaning within biology's theory of evolution, but people often apply the words to any form of competition. The fittest—the strongest, the smartest, the most ruthless—win. They survive because they're just better at the game than all the other poor schlubs out there.

In our world, where money and power and pleasure seem to be the highest goals, many people "win" by cheating. They bend (or completely ignore) the rules. They hold others down in order to elevate themselves. They think, say, and do whatever it takes to gain the upper hand. It should be obvious that this isn't the Christian way.

If you follow Jesus, recognize and reject this *it's all about me* attitude. To avoid regrets,

DON'T DO THIS

Take Advantage of Anyone

When God formed a nation from the family of Abraham, Isaac, and Jacob, He gave the people a lot of rules to follow. The Ten Commandments (Exodus 20:1–17) are the most famous, but there were rules for all sorts of human interactions. Some of these laws were specific to the people of Israel, but all of them point to God's character and desires. Like this one:

> "Never take advantage of poor and destitute laborers, whether they are fellow Israelites or foreigners living in your towns. You must pay them their wages each day before sunset because they are poor and are counting on it. If you don't, they might cry out to the LORD against you, and it would be counted against you as sin." DEUTERONOMY 24:14–15 NLT

God is always concerned about the "little guy" (or girl)—widows, orphans, foreigners, anyone who is weak and susceptible to bullying. But God also demands that we treat *everyone* with fairness, even the "winners" of society:

> "You must not pass along false rumors. You must not cooperate with evil people by lying on the witness stand. You must not follow the crowd in doing wrong. When you are called to testify in a dispute, do not be swayed by the crowd to twist justice. And do not slant your testimony in favor of a person just because that person is poor." EXODUS 23:1–3 NLT

BE *SCRUPULOUS*—ACT IN STRICT REGARD FOR WHAT IS RIGHT.

At times, we're all tempted to take advantage of someone—of our parents' kindness, of a stranger in a business deal, of the girl we're dating. *Don't!* God sees and knows everything we do, and He does have consequences for those who hurt other people. Far better, for everyone involved, to follow that clear, simple rule that Jesus taught:

> **"Do to others as you would like them to do to you."**
> LUKE 6:31 NLT

Lord, what do I gain by taking advantage of others? Only regret. Please help me to be honest and honorable in all my interactions.

26 Do you excel at a sport or musical instrument? Are you really good with electronics or car repairs or landscaping or acting? If someone asked, "What do you do best?" what would you answer?

Next question: Were you as good when you first started as you are now?

Whatever you do well, you've undoubtedly gotten better with practice. No five-year-old straps on skates for the first time and joins the National Hockey League. No second grader gets an Oscar for his performance in a classroom play. No guy sets the world-record high score the first time he picks up a game controller. Sure, some people have natural abilities that might give them a head start. . .but nobody reaches the heights of success without a lot of hard work.

This is also true of the Christian life. Explanation to follow. . .but for now, fix this rule in your mind:

DO THIS
Live by the Spirit

Okay, so your *salvation* doesn't take any work at all—not on your part, at least. Jesus did all the work so you can enjoy all the benefits. When you simply believe He died on a cross as the perfect sacrifice for sin, God saves your soul and adopts you into His family.

But once you're "in," there is work to do. In the process of *sanctification*, you have to deny yourself and do what God's Word says. The responsibility is on you to obey. But the inclination and the power to do right come from the Holy Spirit, the third person of the Trinity, God living in you:

> *Those who are still under the control of their sinful nature can never please God. But you are not controlled by your sinful*

> *nature. You are controlled by the Spirit if you have the Spirit of God living in you.* ROMANS 8:8–9 NLT

GOD GAVE US HIS SPIRIT "TO FILL OUR HEARTS WITH HIS LOVE" (ROMANS 5:5 NLT).

With the Holy Spirit inside, you can do whatever God wants. But because you're still a sinful human being, living in a sinful world, there will be times you choose what *you* want. A true Christian won't continue in sin, though—the Spirit will whisper to your heart and mind, telling you to confess your wrongdoing, to shape up, to get back into fellowship with God.

> *Those who belong to Christ Jesus have nailed the passions and desires of their sinful nature to his cross and crucified them there. Since we are living by the Spirit, let us follow the Spirit's leading in every part of our lives.* GALATIANS 5:24–25 NLT

To "follow the Spirit's leading," read and study God's Word. Pray for wisdom. Listen carefully for what God is saying to your soul. You'll never regret following the Spirit's lead in your life.

Do not stifle the Holy Spirit.
1 THESSALONIANS 5:19 NLT

Holy Spirit, thank You for living within me.
Please guide my thoughts and actions every moment.

27 Every coin has two faces. Here's the flip side to "living by the Spirit."

If you don't live by the Spirit, you're automatically living by the flesh. In the Bible, the word *flesh* often indicates more than just the meat and bones that make up your body—it's your sinful human nature. The "flesh" includes your angry reactions, your lustful thoughts, your lazy moments, your envious desires, your lingering resentments, and so on. Whatever negative feelings plague your life, you can be sure they're part of the flesh.

It's pretty clear that those things cause regret in our lives. That's why it's so important that we

DON'T DO THIS

Live by the Flesh

Until we're born again by surrendering our lives to Jesus, we naturally live by the flesh. Look around, and you'll see a lot of fleshy people doing a lot of fleshy things. Here's how the apostle Paul described them two thousand years ago:

> *The acts of the flesh are obvious: sexual immorality, impurity and debauchery; idolatry and witchcraft; hatred, discord, jealousy, fits of rage, selfish ambition, dissensions, factions and envy; drunkenness, orgies, and the like. I warn you, as I did before, that those who live like this will not inherit the kingdom of God.* GALATIANS 5:19–21 NIV

TRUE SALVATION ALWAYS CREATES LIFE CHANGE.

It's scary to think that a person "will not inherit the kingdom of God." That means eternal separation from God. It's not something that He wants, but it's something His justice demands—especially when people ignore or reject the free gift of salvation that He offers.

But even for those of us who have chosen to follow Jesus, the flesh is still dangerous. Until we're made perfect in heaven, our minds and bodies are continually susceptible to the temptation to sin. And when we willingly and regularly give in to temptation—when we live by the flesh—we're asking for trouble.

> *Do not be deceived: God cannot be mocked. A man reaps what he sows. Whoever sows to please their flesh, from the flesh will reap destruction; whoever sows to please the Spirit, from the Spirit will reap eternal life.* GALATIANS 6:7–8 NIV

This reading has been pretty negative, but don't overlook the positive spin Paul puts on the issue: you can "sow" to please the Spirit, as mentioned above. You can (as he says below) "put to death the misdeeds of the body" and live.

Don't let the flesh control your life. Allowing God's Spirit to guide your thoughts, words, and actions truly will make everything better.

If you live according to the flesh, you will die; but if by the Spirit you put to death the misdeeds of the body, you will live.
ROMANS 8:13 NIV

Lord, my flesh wants all kinds of stuff that You say no to. Strengthen me by Your Spirit to obey Your Word. I want to avoid the sin that will cause regret.

28 The United States' third president, Thomas Jefferson (the guy on the nickel), assembled a list of twelve life rules that he passed along to his children and grandchildren. His "Canons of Conduct" included sayings like "Never spend your money before you have it," "We never repent of having eaten too little," and "When angry, count to 10 before you speak; if very angry, 100."

What rule was number one? "Never put off to tomorrow what you can do today." Clever guy, that Tom Jefferson. He knew that avoiding duties—big or small—can lead to disappointment and regret. So he made sure to take care of that rule first.

In our pursuit of a no-regrets life, we can boil Jefferson's principle down to this:

DON'T DO THIS
Procrastinate

Like so many words, *procrastinate* comes from Latin: it's a combination of *pro-* (meaning "forward") and *crastinus* (meaning "of tomorrow"). When you push important things forward, into tomorrow, you fall behind. Make that a habit, and it looks a lot like laziness.

You won't find the word (or even forms of it) in most Bible translations, though it's in a headline in the New King James Version: FELIX PROCRASTINATES. Here's the scene with that Roman governor, from the New Life Version:

> *Paul spoke about being right with God. He spoke about being the boss over our own desires. He spoke about standing before One Who will tell us if we are guilty. When Felix heard this, he became afraid and said, "Go now. I will send for you when it is a better time."* ACTS 24:25 NLV

"I will. . .when it is a better time." Even without using the term *procrastination*, the Bible shows it in action. But why is procrastination a problem? Well, if it's based in laziness, that's not at all like God, who is "working all the time" (John 5:17 NLV). It's also foolish to put things off, because nobody—not even a teen guy—knows how much life he has left:

> Listen! You who say, "Today or tomorrow we will go to this city and stay a year and make money." You do not know about tomorrow. What is your life? It is like fog. You see it and soon it is gone. JAMES 4:13–14 NLV

ALSO A GOOD WARNING AGAINST PRIDE

Procrastination derails our personal growth, our relationships, and our service to God, making us less than we should be. Fight it—right now.

> *You must warn each other every day, while it is still "today," so that none of you will be deceived by sin and hardened against God.*
> HEBREWS 3:13 NLT

It's always tempting, Lord, to put off the important things of life. But I know You call me to work and serve and do more than coast. Please give me the wisdom and strength to banish procrastination.

29 If your house is burning, you hope there's a fire station nearby. It's great if the firefighters are well trained, physically fit, and familiar with the construction of your home. You want them to drive properly maintained, newer-model trucks with all the best firefighting technology. And, as a bonus, it's cool if your local crew has won the Firefighters' Challenge at the state fair for the past three years.

But none of that matters if they don't come when you call.

Here's an important rule for life, whether you're a firefighter or not:

DO THIS

Show Up

Even if your local department lacks top-of-the-line skills and equipment, you still want them in your time of need. Far better to have *some* help in your moment of crisis than none at all.

At times you'll be called on to "put out a fire" in other people's lives—they'll need help with certain crises, whether emotional or physical or financial or whatever. When that call comes, don't ignore it. To avoid regret later, get up and help now—no matter how difficult or inconvenient it may be. Here's a scripture specifically about helping fellow believers out of sin—but the principle really applies to every aspect of life:

> *Carry each other's burdens, and in this way you will fulfill the law of Christ.* GALATIANS 6:2 NIV

YOUR FAITH ISN'T ALL ABOUT YOU.

When family and friends, your classmates, and fellow Christians need you, be sure to show up for them. But show up for yourself too.

What does that mean? When you take a job, no matter how mundane or uninspiring it may be, show up—every time you're scheduled. When it's time for class at school, show up—both physically and mentally. Even if it's easier to sleep in than to head out to church on Sunday, show up. If there's a family event that doesn't thrill you, show up anyway.

Why? Because the discipline of doing hard things will serve you well throughout life. You know how adults like to say, "It builds character"? Well, they're right.

> *We also glory in our sufferings, because we know that suffering produces perseverance; perseverance, character; and character, hope.* Romans 5:3–4 NIV

Many grown men look back on their younger years and say, "Man, I wish I would have worked harder. . .goofed off less. . .stayed on top of my relationships. . .used my time and talents more carefully." Since you're still young, you have the perfect opportunity to avoid that kind of regret. Just make sure you show up.

Then I heard the voice of the Lord saying, "Whom shall I send? And who will go for us?" And I said, "Here am I. Send me!"
Isaiah 6:8 NIV

Lord Jesus, You showed up for me. Now please help me to show up too—for others and myself.

30 Jocks, by nature, are aggressive. They want to win. They want to outscore, outperform, outclass their competition. They want the thrill of victory for themselves—and the agony of defeat for the other guys. That's just the nature of athletics.

And yet there's still the old-fashioned notion of sportsmanship, those unwritten guidelines that say you play by the rules, respect your opponent, and win gracefully. A story is told of the great Green Bay Packers coach Vince Lombardi, who dumped cold water (figuratively speaking) on a kick returner's touchdown celebration. "The next time you make it to the end zone," the coach muttered, "act like you've been there before."

Which leads us into a good rule for a no-regrets life:

DON'T DO THIS
Show Off

Isn't it kind of embarrassing to see a tackle celebrating a stop he made with his team down by 21? But it's not only athletes who show off.

Ever known a guy who bragged about his hot car, his cool home, his superior grades, his cheerleader girlfriend? Have *you* ever done that? It's a great way to push people away, both from yourself and from the God you serve.

Better to follow the example of John the Baptist. Centuries before he was born, John had been prophesied as the forerunner of the Messiah, the Savior whom God would send into the world (Isaiah 40:3; Matthew 3:3). When Jesus went public, He said, "I tell you, of all who have ever lived, none is greater than John" (Luke 7:28 NLT). But rather than spike the ball or cut a rug in the end zone, John said,

> *"He must become greater and greater, and I must become less and less."* JOHN 3:30 NLT

A GREAT PERSPECTIVE FOR ALL OF US

Showing off, boasting, thinking we're better than others—these are all relationship killers. And God made every one of us to want and need people in our lives.

Whatever gifts you have—looks, brains, talent, money—they all come from God. And He expects you to use them for His purposes, not your own. Even the "best" people are still just people, and the apostle Paul has wise advice:

> *Because of the privilege and authority God has given me, I give each of you this warning: Don't think you are better than you really are. Be honest in your evaluation of yourselves, measuring yourselves by the faith God has given us.* ROMANS 12:3 NLT

If you want to impress people, don't show off. Be compassionate and helpful. You, they, and God will be pleased.

> *"Those who wish to boast should boast in this alone:*
> *that they truly know me and understand that I am*
> *the LORD who demonstrates unfailing love and who*
> *brings justice and righteousness to the earth, and that*
> *I delight in these things. I, the LORD, have spoken!"*
> JEREMIAH 9:24 NLT

Lord, I want to find my affirmation in You.
May I impress others with my humble service.

31 It's a sensitive subject, so we'll drop our voices for a moment and discuss. . .sex.

Nothing graphic or inappropriate, of course. But since it's a major source of regret in our world, how can we not consider the dangers of this crazy obsession?

When used properly, like a prescription medication, sex is good—very good. "Used properly" means "enjoyed with your wife in a committed marriage relationship." But anything beyond that, according to God's Word, is trouble.

When you have an opportunity to engage in sex outside of a God-honoring marriage, here's the rule:

DO THIS

Get Up and Go

What do I mean? Just this: *Run!* If you're tempted by sexual stuff on the internet, get up and go away from your device. If your mind is wandering toward lustful thoughts, get up and go—somewhere, anywhere you can take a few breaths and reset your thinking. If you're with a girl and things are getting out of hand, get up and go like Joseph, the favored son of Jacob sold into slavery by his jealous older brothers:

> *Joseph was a very handsome and well-built young man, and Potiphar's wife soon began to look at him lustfully. "Come and sleep with me," she demanded.*
>
> *But Joseph refused. "Look," he told her, "my master trusts me with everything in his entire household. No one here has more authority than I do. He has held back nothing from me except you, because you are his wife. How could I do such a wicked thing? It would be a great sin against God."*

She kept putting pressure on Joseph day after day, but he refused to sleep with her, and he kept out of her way as much as possible. One day, however, no one else was around when he went in to do his work. She came and grabbed him by his cloak, demanding, "Come on, sleep with me!" Joseph tore himself away, but he left his cloak in her hand as he ran from the house. GENESIS 39:6–12 NLT

HOW OFTEN DO MOVIES OR TV SHOWS PORTRAY A GUY LIKE JOSEPH?

When temptation knocks on the front door, run out the back—remove yourself from the premises. Is that easy? No. Might it cause other issues? Yes. Potiphar's wife, furious that Joseph had resisted her advances, accused him of trying to rape her, and he went to prison for years. That must have been very disappointing, but regret over sexual sin was not among Joseph's sorrows.

Don't let it be among yours either.

God's will is for you to be holy, so stay away from all sexual sin. Then each of you will control his own body and live in holiness and honor—not in lustful passion like the pagans who do not know God and his ways.

1 THESSALONIANS 4:3–5 NLT

Lord, help me to stand apart from this world, keeping my mind and body pure for the woman I'll marry someday.

32 Life expectancy for the average American guy, according to government statistics, is 73.5 years. That's around 26,846 days.

Seventy-some years? Almost twenty-seven thousand days? Sounds like a long haul. But consider this: by the time you turn fifteen, you've already burned 20 percent of the typical male life span. One day you'll wake up and realize you're twenty-five. . .forty. . .sixty. Life really does move that fast.

You have a lot of things to pack into your time on earth. Avoid regrets of the worst sort by making sure God tops your list.

DON'T DO THIS
Disregard God

The fact that you're reading this book indicates you believe in God—or are willing to consider Him. What you read here and in the pages of His Word supports what anyone can "read" in the book of creation—the incredible physical world of stars and planets and light, of mountains and rivers and trees, of lions and bees and platypuses.

Yet it's possible—even common—for people to disregard God. We get distracted by other things, we think we have better plans for our lives, we [fill in the blank with your favorite excuse]. But a day is coming when God will take away people's choice, and He'll demand the honor He deserves from everyone:

> *So when the name of Jesus is spoken, everyone in heaven and on earth and under the earth will bow down before Him. And every tongue will say Jesus Christ is Lord. Everyone will give honor to God the Father.* PHILIPPIANS 2:10–11 NLV

You can bow now or bow later. You'll bow either way, so why not do it immediately, willingly, and enjoy all the benefits of knowing God? When He says this world's time is up, those who have ignored, mocked, and hated God will realize how wrong they were—but too late.

Hopefully, none of us are in that disregarding crowd. But even guys who go to church and identify as Christians should ask themselves what they're really trusting in. Here's a disturbing thought from Jesus:

> "Not everyone who says to me, 'Lord, Lord,' will enter the kingdom of heaven, but only the one who does the will of my Father who is in heaven." MATTHEW 7:21 NIV

MAKE SURE YOU'RE "IN."

It's true: even self-professed Christians can disregard God, missing the real point of this life to their eternal regret. That's frightening, but absolutely avoidable. Jesus was very clear about His Father's will, which opens the door to heaven: "The work of God is this: to believe in the one he has sent" (John 6:29 NIV).

My brothers and sisters, make every effort to confirm your calling and election. . . . And you will receive a rich welcome into the eternal kingdom of our Lord and Savior Jesus Christ.
2 PETER 1:10–11 NIV

Draw me close, Father, through Your Son, Jesus Christ. May I focus my entire life on You.

33 In the 1948 US presidential election, incumbent Democrat Harry S. Truman faced a strong challenge from the Republican governor of New York, Thomas Dewey. Many people believed Dewey would easily defeat Truman, the former vice president who rose to power when Franklin D. Roosevelt died in office. But the conventional wisdom was false—Truman earned a comfortable win.

On election night, the strongly Republican *Chicago Daily Tribune* had an early press deadline. Lacking final vote counts from the entire country, the editors decided to run with a prepackaged story and headline celebrating their candidate's presumed victory. But 150,000 copies of the DEWEY DEFEATS TRUMAN edition proved to be wrong, and in one of the more famous photos of American history, a laughing Truman holds up the fake-news newspaper. It's now a collector's item.

When we make a mistake like that—not paying attention, making bad assumptions, speaking too soon—it's nothing we want to hold on to. To avoid that kind of regret, here's a good rule:

DO THIS

Listen First, Speak Later

Have you ever popped off and said something dumb without knowing what you were talking about? (Who hasn't?) Quick, careless words can embarrass us, to be sure, but even worse, they can really hurt other people. God's heart is for hope and healing, so He gives us some very clear instructions about our speech:

> *My dear brothers and sisters, take note of this: Everyone should be quick to listen, slow to speak and slow to become angry.* JAMES 1:19 NIV

ANOTHER GREAT VERSE TO MEMORIZE!

God knows what we're going to say even before we speak the words (see Psalm 139:4). This "omniscience," His all-knowingness, is one of the amazing characteristics of God. Obviously, we don't have that kind of knowledge, so we need to stop and really listen to what other people are saying.

Maybe a friend has worked up the courage to tell you about a problem that's really bothering him. But rather than hearing him out, you pass judgment or jump right into some (probably unhelpful) advice. When that happens, you've missed a huge opportunity—to really help someone you care about and deepen your friendship.

> *Do you see someone who speaks in haste? There is more hope for a fool than for them.* PROVERBS 29:20 NIV

Ask any adult—they probably recall many times when they spoke too quickly or without knowledge and then wished they hadn't. Learn from them—and from the *Chicago Daily Tribune*. Head off those DEWEY DEFEATS TRUMAN moments before they even start.

> *Those who consider themselves religious and yet do not keep a tight rein on their tongues deceive themselves, and their religion is worthless.*
> JAMES 1:26 NIV

Lord, forgive me for the times I've spoken too quickly and carelessly. Open my ears and control my mouth so I speak only what is helpful.

34 Dietrich Bonhoeffer, a Lutheran pastor in Germany, watched Adolf Hitler and his National Socialist Party rise to power. As a leading voice opposing the Nazis, Bonhoeffer was ultimately arrested and executed days before Germany surrendered in World War II. He was only thirty-nine years old.

Followers of Jesus perform for an audience of one: God Himself. Though His is the only opinion that matters, even many unbelievers will ultimately respect a Christian who does the right thing. Decades after his death, Bonhoeffer is widely admired; church people who supported the Nazis are held in disdain.

Others may or may not recognize your good behavior, but God certainly does. To avoid regrets, always do what He tells you.

DO THIS

Stand Up for What's Right

The classic Bible story of Shadrach, Meshach, and Abednego tells of young men who stood up for God—literally and figuratively. These intelligent and good-looking guys had been taken from their homes when Babylon overran Judah. Now, in the service of King Nebuchadnezzar, they came up against his crazy demand to bow in worship before a giant golden statue. They said no.

> At this time some astrologers came forward and denounced the Jews. They said to King Nebuchadnezzar, "May the king live forever! Your Majesty has issued a decree that everyone who hears the sound of the horn, flute, zither, lyre, harp, pipe and all kinds of music must fall down and worship the image of gold, and that whoever does not fall down and worship will be thrown into a blazing furnace. But there are some Jews whom you have set over the affairs of the

province of Babylon—Shadrach, Meshach and Abednego—
who pay no attention to you, Your Majesty. They neither
serve your gods nor worship the image of gold you have
set up." DANIEL 3:8–12 NIV

TALK ABOUT GUTS!

Unlike Bonhoeffer, these young men survived their attempted execution, as God protected them in the superheated furnace. But as with the German pastor, they go down in history as heroes, believers who obeyed God and set an example of standing up for what's right.

The stakes will probably be lower for us. But the expectation is exactly the same:

So then, brothers and sisters, stand firm and hold fast to the
teachings we passed on to you, whether by word of mouth
or by letter. 2 THESSALONIANS 2:15 NIV

Standing up is hard. But bowing to the demands of culture is no option. For a no-regrets life, you'll need both supportive Christian friends and a clean heart that's open to God's leading. Oh, and don't forget this:

Put on the full armor of God, so that when the day
of evil comes, you may be able to stand your ground,
and after you have done everything, to stand.
EPHESIANS 6:13 NIV

Stiffen my spine, Father, so I can stand
tall for You in every situation.

35 Many years have passed, and Marc is still embarrassed by his college debut. No, he didn't trip in front of a pretty girl or set the chemistry lab on fire. For the first two days, he just sat in his dorm room, scared to go out and be part of things.

What scares you? For some people, it's spiders. For others, germs. Others, the future. One guy is afraid his girlfriend will leave him. Another guy fears climate change. The next guy is terrified of God.

Scary things come in all shapes and sizes, seemingly tailor-made for your personality. Satan uses them to keep you defeated and ineffective as a Christian—and that leads to big regrets. But it's certainly not God's plan for His children. Here's the biblical rule:

DON'T DO THIS

Live in Fear

Granted, there may be clinical phobias that require counseling and possibly medication to overcome. But a lot of our fears are just minor challenges that we can and should work to defeat. Ever hear what the apostle Paul told his "son in the faith," Timothy?

> *God has not given us a spirit of fear and timidity, but of power, love, and self-discipline.* 2 TIMOTHY 1:7 NLT

In context, Paul wanted Timothy to be confident in his ministry, never "ashamed to tell others about our Lord" (2 Timothy 1:8 NLT). But the words truly apply to all of life.

Some people say the Bible contains enough "fear not" passages for each day of the year. Perhaps. But in the New Living Translation there are definitely 65 instances of "don't be afraid" and another 36 instances of "do not be afraid"—a nice, round 101 courage boosters, straight from God Himself.

Why should fear have no hold on Christians? Because, as Joshua was told, "the LORD your God is with you wherever you go" (Joshua 1:9 NLT). For New Testament confirmation, Jesus promised, "I am with you always, even to the end of the age" (Matthew 28:20 NLT).

Jesus had a very interesting comment on fear:

> *"Dear friends, don't be afraid of those who want to kill your body; they cannot do any more to you after that. But I'll tell you whom to fear. Fear God, who has the power to kill you and then throw you into hell. Yes, he's the one to fear."* LUKE 12:4–5 NLT

JESUS NEVER HESITATED TO WARN SINNERS.

Remember that guy afraid of God? It's a legitimate fear until he believes in Jesus and becomes "accepted in the Beloved" (Ephesians 1:6 SKJV). If that's you, don't waste your time and energy being afraid. If not, why not settle the issue with God right now?

"Don't be afraid, for I am with you. Don't be discouraged, for I am your God. I will strengthen you and help you."
ISAIAH 41:10 NLT

This can be a scary world, Lord, but I know You're in control. Please give me courage to face my fears.

36 Are you a generally positive or negative guy? Do you see the proverbial glass as half-empty or half-full? When you're taking a test, applying for a job, or asking a girl for a date, do you expect good things? Or disaster?

Part of our outlook on life comes from the basic personality God gave us. Part of our natural, everyday outlook on life may arise from our own experiences, both good and bad. But for any guy who follows Jesus, there should be a desire to see the bright side of things. Don't regret a negativity that drags you (and the people around you) down. Instead,

DO THIS

Look Up

This is no "positive thinking" gimmick that says you can bend the universe to your will with the right mindset. It's an acknowledgment that you have an awesome helper above who wants the very best for you. And this helper has infinite wisdom and absolute power to make "the best for you" happen.

> *I lift up my eyes to the mountains—where does my help come from? My help comes from the Lord, the Maker of heaven and earth.* PSALM 121:1–2 NIV

With that kind of help from that kind of God, you *should* think positively. You should be optimistic. You should see the glass as *totally* full. Why believe the sky is falling when God the Father sent His Son, Jesus, to pay the price for your sins? Now that you've been saved by grace through faith, look up!

> *Since, then, you have been raised with Christ, set your hearts on things above, where Christ is, seated at the right hand of*

God. Set your minds on things above, not on earthly things.
COLOSSIANS 3:1–2 NIV

CHRISTIANS SHOULD ALWAYS EMPHASIZE "HIGHER" THINGS.

Looking up doesn't guarantee you'll ace the test, get the job, or sweep the girl off her feet. You still need to study, interview well, and maintain good (okay, *excellent*) hygiene. But if you've done your part, you can trust that God will do His. . .that whatever happens will be His best for you, even if that's different from what you originally hoped.

You'll regret keeping your eyes down, on this cursed earth. Followers of Jesus should always look up.

Finally, brothers and sisters, whatever is true, whatever is noble, whatever is right, whatever is pure, whatever is lovely, whatever is admirable—if anything is excellent or praiseworthy—think about such things. Whatever you have learned or received or heard from me, or seen in me—put it into practice. And the God of peace will be with you.
PHILIPPIANS 4:8–9 NIV

I have every reason for hope, Lord, because You promise me Your presence now and forever. If I ever forget that, please remind me of Your amazing love.

37

For a guy born in the 1930s, he's looking good: Superman is as ripped as ever.

Check that, even more ripped.

The brainchild of young Clevelanders Jerry Siegel and Joe Shuster, Superman debuted in *Action Comics* in 1938. The "Man of Steel" was impervious to bullets, able to jump skyscrapers, capable of outrunning fast trains and seeing through walls. To a nation facing the depressing realities of the Great Depression, the invincible Superman was an upbeat symbol of better things.

Before long, though, we learned that even Superman had vulnerabilities—chief among them, green Kryptonite, an element from his home planet. When the bad guys got hold of that, Supe was suddenly very. . .human.

Which leads us to an observation for a no-regrets life:

DON'T DO THIS
Think You're Invincible

Teens often think they're immune to the laws of nature—that they'll never wreck a speeding motorcycle, for example, or get punched in the nose for mouthing off to the wrong guy. Sadly, many think they're immune to spiritual laws too and, over time, find themselves addicted to alcohol or drugs or pornography.

For a no-regrets life, never think you're invincible. In fact, tell yourself often that, apart from God's grace, you could seriously crash and burn when Satan shows up with your own personal Kryptonite.

Watch yourself! The person who thinks he can stand against sin had better watch that he does not fall into sin. 1 Corinthians 10:12 NLV

In context, the apostle Paul was saying that guys who want to help fellow believers out of sin need to be careful—they might be tempted to sin themselves, succumbing to either the problem their friend is fighting or perhaps pride, thinking they're better than the other guy. If it's so easy to fall when you're doing something *good*, how much easier must it be if you're just killing time, by yourself or with other bored people?

Let's check with Paul again:

> *Be careful how you live. Live as men who are wise and not foolish. Make the best use of your time. These are sinful days.*
> EPHESIANS 5:15–16 NLV

GOD'S WORD MAKES US WISE—PSALM 19:7.

When it comes to sin, nobody—and I mean *nobody*—is invincible. Stay alert and pray (all the time) for God's wisdom and protection. As you do, you'll gain a certain type of invincibility—the knowledge that nothing on earth can harm you until God says your time is up. Let's give Paul the final word:

> *I desire to depart and be with Christ, which is better by far;*
> *but it is more necessary for you that I remain in the body.*
> *Convinced of this, I know that I will remain, and I will continue*
> *with all of you for your progress and joy in the faith.*
> PHILIPPIANS 1:23–25 NIV

Remind me every day, Lord, of the dangers of sin.
I am vulnerable, but You can protect me.

38 Seems like everyone wants to be an influencer these days. Got an interest and a cell phone? Post your passion online—and if you can draw an audience, you can make some serious bucks. Whether you're all about world travel, fancy cuisine, video gaming, or shredding the electric guitar, you can become an internet celebrity. You can influence others to join your personal cause.

You know where this is going, right?

What cause could be greater than sharing the good news about Jesus? The things of this world are passing away, and fast. You'll regret not keeping your focus on the most important thing. Here's a rule to tape across your phone screen:

DO THIS

Be an Influencer—for Eternity

Want to know something cool? You can actually use your interests on earth to help share heaven. Really—your zeal for travel, your taste for fine cooking, your passion for video games or guitars can be a tool for reaching people who don't yet know Jesus. Find that common ground, developing relationships that allow you to speak to the most important issue of all: the question of eternal life.

The apostle Paul wasn't talking about hobbies and pastimes, but he knew how to meet people exactly where they were:

> Though I am free and belong to no one, I have made myself a slave to everyone, to win as many as possible. To the Jews I became like a Jew, to win the Jews. To those under the law I became like one under the law (though I myself am not under the law), so as to win those under the law. To those not having the law I became like one not having the law (though I am not free from God's law but am under Christ's law), so as to win

those not having the law. To the weak I became weak, to win the weak. I have become all things to all people so that by all possible means I might save some. 1 CORINTHIANS 9:19–22 NIV

TECHNOLOGY IS GREAT, BUT NOTHING BEATS PERSONAL INTERACTION.

If you're a Christian, you know the ultimate truth—Jesus Himself—that the world so desperately needs. So today and every day, pray for strength to live out your faith—and the courage to speak the truth to others. This is serious business:

Be merciful to those who doubt; save others by snatching them from the fire. JUDE 22–23 NIV

When you influence others for eternity—when you point them to their Creator and Redeemer, Jesus—there will be no regrets at all. Just a long, long, long celebration in His presence.

"Those who are wise will shine like the brightness
of the heavens, and those who lead many to
righteousness, like the stars for ever and ever."
DANIEL 12:3 NIV

Lord, I want to influence others for good—
for You. Use me to speak Your truth.

39 At a large public university, theater majors performed a play for incoming freshmen and their parents. As part of the official orientation, actors depicted the "college experience" new students could expect.

There were stern warnings against cigarette smoking. There were halfhearted warnings against alcohol and drugs—but since students were obviously going to use them anyway, they were urged, "Make sure you have a designated driver."

Then the topic turned to sex. Were there warnings? No. In fact, experimentation of every sort was encouraged—enthusiastically. Many parents left the theater thinking, *That was weird. . . .*

Weird but common. In a culture that sets minimum ages for driving, getting tattoos, and joining the army, sexual things are pushed on younger and younger kids all the time. The potential regrets are immense, so

DON'T DO THIS
Jump into Sex

God created sex for good purposes—intimacy in marriage and the creation of families. But Satan has warped it, turning sex into a selfish pleasure-chase very different from its intended meaning. Unplanned pregnancies and sexually transmitted diseases are among its regrets. But because sex outside of marriage shows contempt for God, it can also lead to emotional and spiritual problems.

Proverbs urges young men to obey their father's teaching—which should be God's teaching—regarding sex:

> *It will keep you from the immoral woman, from the smooth tongue of a promiscuous woman. Don't lust for her beauty. Don't let her coy glances seduce you. For a prostitute will*

> *bring you to poverty, but sleeping with another man's wife will cost you your life. Can a man scoop a flame into his lap and not have his clothes catch on fire? Can he walk on hot coals and not blister his feet?* PROVERBS 6:24–28 NLT

The burning analogy is interesting. Like flaming logs in a fireplace, sex in a committed marriage is a great thing. But if those logs roll out of the fireplace—if you're having sex outside of God's rules—your house can burn down.

It's not just the physical act that's dangerous. Jesus had strong words regarding our eyes and minds:

> *"You have heard the commandment that says, 'You must not commit adultery.' But I say, anyone who even looks at a woman with lust has already committed adultery with her in his heart."* MATTHEW 5:27–28 NLT

A STRONG WARNING AGAINST PORN...

When it comes to sex, your best approach is "wait"—for marriage with that perfect girl. If you've already been sexually active, know that God will forgive any sin you confess. But then go back to "wait."

Give honor to marriage, and remain faithful to one another in marriage. God will surely judge people who are immoral and those who commit adultery.

HEBREWS 13:4 NLT

This world pushes sex all the time, Lord. Help me to see through the lies to Your perfect plan for sex within marriage. Keep me pure, I pray, for my future wife.

40 How many times have you witnessed a rude interaction, either in person or online? Probably too many to count. How many times have you *engaged* in a rude interaction?

Uh, next question, please.

There's no doubt that people are frustrating. They brag on themselves and belittle us. They steal our time and peace and ideas and give us blame in return. They seem bound and determined to provoke us to anger and some crazy overreaction.

And then, when we give in, we regret it.

As Christians, we know we should do better. Deep down inside, God's Spirit is always whispering,

DO THIS

Live by the Golden Rule

All through history, many cultures and religions have had a form of the Golden Rule. Because people are sinful and selfish by nature, the rule often took a negative form: *Don't do to other people what you don't want them doing to you.* That makes sense, of course. But when Jesus walked the earth, He put a different, more positive spin on things:

> *"Do to others whatever you would like them to do to you. This is the essence of all that is taught in the law and the prophets."* MATTHEW 7:12 NLT

IT DOESN'T GET MUCH CLEARER THAN THAT.

If you want to be respected, show respect to others. If you like to be treated with kindness, sow seeds of friendliness, helpfulness, and generousness (also known as generosity). If you hope for peace with your fellow man and woman, guys and girls, answer all of their irritating, idiotic instigations with a cool, calm, and collected *Christian* response. In other words, be like Jesus.

> *"Love your enemies! Do good to them. Lend to them without expecting to be repaid. Then your reward from heaven will be very great, and you will truly be acting as children of the Most High, for he is kind to those who are unthankful and wicked."* LUKE 6:35 NLT

Now, let's be clear: following the Golden Rule doesn't guarantee that others will treat you well. Jesus Himself was hated by many and ultimately killed. Chances are a lot of people will be just as mean and obnoxious as ever. But your kindness might shock some of them into better behavior, and even cause them to ask why you're different.

Then God, who will certainly reward your good behavior, just might draw those people into His family. There will never be regret when you treat people with kindness.

> *Keep your tongue from speaking evil and your lips from telling lies! Turn away from evil and do good. Search for peace, and work to maintain it.*
> PSALM 34:13–14 NLT

Lord Jesus, help me to live by Your Golden Rule. May I treat other people the way I'd like to be treated—and may they always see You in me.

41 Did you see Elon Musk's big rocket go boom in 2023?

The SpaceX *Starship*, said to be the most powerful rocket ever built, exploded just minutes into its April 20, 2023, flight. Well, check that—SpaceX said it wasn't an explosion but rather a "rapid unscheduled disassembly."

Dictionary.com responded with a tweet: "We're pretty good with synonyms, but 'rapid unscheduled disassembly' is a new one, even for us."

This was all tongue in cheek. But while some had fun with an expensive failure, we can take a life lesson from it:

DO THIS

Say What You Mean

Consciously telling untruths can cause us regret. Lying to gain advantage over others inevitably brings guilt and consequences to a follower of Jesus. But even shading the truth to save a person's feelings may come back to haunt us—dishonesty has a way of mutating and metastasizing into something we never intended.

Plain, straightforward speech is your best policy. Here's what Jesus says:

> "You have heard that it was said to the people long ago, 'Do not break your oath, but fulfill to the Lord the vows you have made.' But I tell you, do not swear an oath at all: either by heaven, for it is God's throne; or by the earth, for it is his footstool; or by Jerusalem, for it is the city of the Great King. And do not swear by your head, for you cannot make even one hair white or black. All you need to say is simply 'Yes' or 'No'; anything beyond this comes from the evil one."
> MATTHEW 5:33–37 NIV

Look at what the apostle Paul included in his list of personal behaviors that helped point people to God:

> *We put no stumbling block in anyone's path, so that our ministry will not be discredited. Rather, as servants of God we commend ourselves in every way: in great endurance; in troubles, hardships and distresses; in beatings, imprisonments and riots; in hard work, sleepless nights and hunger; in purity, understanding, patience and kindness; in the Holy Spirit and in sincere love; in truthful speech.* 2 CORINTHIANS 6:3–7 NIV

SINCE GOD IS TRUE, HIS KIDS MUST BE TOO.

Of course, we should always speak the truth gently, and there's often a place for good humor. Just be careful: don't ever let knowingly false words cause your own rapid unscheduled disassembly.

> *Each of you must put off falsehood and speak truthfully to your neighbor, for we are all members of one body.*
> EPHESIANS 4:25 NIV

It's so easy to shade the truth, Lord Jesus—to lie. I want to make myself look better, to keep others from being disappointed, to gain some kind of personal advantage. Please help me to be like You, speaking the truth in love, every time and everywhere.

42 Mick was doing a good deed—a really good deed. He had volunteered to paint an elderly neighbor lady's home.

Since it was a small, one-story ranch, Mick wouldn't face dizzying heights. But he would have to use a ladder, and he knew he'd be up and down a million times. Mick would paint as far as he could reach then slide the ladder a couple of feet and repeat the process. This was going to take awhile.

He'd just started when a man walked across the yard. "I'm Catherine's pastor—thanks for helping her out," he told Mick. "Hey, I have another ladder and some jacks that might help you—if you set up the ladders parallel to each other, you can lay a board on the jacks between them. You can work from the platform and you won't have to move your one ladder so often."

That sounded good. But Mick wasn't sure if he should accept. Maybe he didn't want to trouble the pastor. Maybe it was just silly pride that wanted to say, "Oh no, I'm fine!" Whatever the case, the story points to a good rule for a no-regrets life:

DON'T DO THIS
Refuse Help

After a quick internal debate, Mick made a good choice. "That sounds really helpful," he said. "I'd love that." The setup worked beautifully, and the project went faster than he expected.

Most of us prefer to be independent. But if someone cares enough to offer a hand, why say no? Do you recall the story of Philip, who was prompted by God's Spirit to speak to an Ethiopian official visiting Jerusalem?

Philip ran up to the chariot and heard the man reading Isaiah the prophet. "Do you understand what you are reading?"

> *Philip asked. "How can I," he said, "unless someone explains it to me?" So he invited Philip to come up and sit with him.* ACTS 8:30–31 NIV

The Ethiopian became a Christian that day because he was willing to accept help. Had he said, "No, thanks—I can figure this out myself," where would he be now?

Accepting help is good for us but also for the person helping. The apostle Paul received financial aid from Christians in Philippi, telling them that while Jesus took care of him in every circumstance,

> *It was good of you to share in my troubles. . . . Not that I desire your gifts; what I desire is that more be credited to your account.* PHILIPPIANS 4:14, 17 NIV

THINK OF THAT: GOD "CREDITS YOUR ACCOUNT" WHEN YOU HELP OTHERS.

Don't make your own life harder by refusing help. And never prevent others from enjoying the rewards of helping.

> *The gifts you sent. . .are a fragrant offering,*
> *an acceptable sacrifice, pleasing to God.*
> PHILIPPIANS 4:18 NIV

Lord, if nobody accepts, how can anyone help anyone else? May I never refuse help out of pride.

43 Before Aaron Judge and Bryce Harper, before Shohei Ohtani and Mike Trout, there was Ernie Banks. Chosen as one of thirty best major-league players of the twentieth century, he defined talent and class in baseball from 1953 to 1971 and was elected to the Hall of Fame in his first year of eligibility.

Banks, who played his entire career with the generally weak Chicago Cubs, finished with 512 home runs and 2,583 hits. He was an All-Star fourteen times and won the National League Most Valuable Player Award twice—on Cubs teams that played sub-.500 ball. Though he never got to play in the postseason, Ernie Banks was famed for his upbeat personality and cheery catchphrase, "It's a beautiful day for a ball game—let's play two!" People called him "Mr. Sunshine."

It's so easy to complain and criticize, to grumble, whine, and moan. Why not take a tip from Ernie Banks and

DO THIS
Be Mr. Positive

Out of all the people on earth, Christians should be the most upbeat. Not because our lives are easy—don't forget that Jesus, Peter, and Paul all *guaranteed* us hardship (see John 16:33; 1 Peter 4:12–13; and 2 Timothy 3:12). But we have God's promises—not only of His help in this life but of a perfect, eternal life to come. We'll ultimately regret focusing on our disappointments, overlooking the love and power that are always available to us:

> "For I am the Lord your God Who holds your right hand, and Who says to you, 'Do not be afraid. I will help you.' " ISAIAH 41:13 NLV

And think about this: If we as Christians complain and mumble and mope around, why would anyone want to join God's family? That's the most important decision people can make. . .but when we're crabby and critical, we can quickly push others away from the Lord.

The apostle Peter urged us to be like Jesus, patiently enduring the insults and attacks of those who hate Him (1 Peter 2:19–23). That will ultimately have a surprising and beneficial effect on them:

> *When you are around people who do not know God, be careful how you act. Even if they talk against you as wrong-doers, in the end they will give thanks to God for your good works when Christ comes again.* 1 PETER 2:12 NLV

GIVE IT TIME—THE TRUTH ALWAYS WINS.

This world has enough negativity without us as Christians adding to it. Take a different path, the no-regrets road. Be Mr. Positive.

Worry in the heart of a man weighs it down,
but a good word makes it glad.
PROVERBS 12:25 NLV

Lord Jesus, You have given me every reason to be upbeat—my sins are forgiven and my future is secure. Thank You for promising to be with me. Now help me to share Your good news with everyone else.

44 And now for a quick quiz: What do the following have in common? (1) Sugar. (2) Gold. (3) Petroleum. (4) Table salt. (5) Copper. (6) Flour. (7) You.

Answer: They all go through a refining process.

Refining is the method of freeing various materials from impurities. Metals are often refined by the application of heat—lots of heat. People are refined in much the same way.

The process isn't fun, and there will be times when you just want to run away. But the process has purpose, and short-circuiting what God is doing in your life will create regret. So here's a good rule of thumb:

DON'T DO THIS
Resist the Refining

God will use any number of people, situations, and personal struggles to refine you, to free you from the undesirable aspects of your being. (We *all* have them.) Maybe you've felt the incredible heat and pressure of His refining process already. If you haven't, just wait—it will come. But don't dread what God is trying to accomplish.

> *My brothers, count it all joy when you fall into various temptations, knowing this, that the trying of your faith works patience. But let patience have her perfect work, that you may be perfect and complete, lacking nothing.* JAMES 1:2–4 SKJV

COUNT = "CONSIDER"

When you believe in Jesus, you are saved from the penalty of your sins and set on the path toward heaven. But you still live in a messed-up world, and God will use its frustrations and disappointments and outright tragedies to make you more like your Lord—submissive, patient, compassionate.

The author of the book of James—who may have been a half brother of Jesus—said we should consider our refining a joyful process. Peter, who was one of Jesus' closest companions, saw the process the same way:

> *In this you greatly rejoice, though now for a season, if need be, you are in heaviness through many different temptations, that the trial of your faith, being much more precious than gold that perishes, though it is tried with fire, might be found to praise and honor and glory at the appearing of Jesus Christ.*
> 1 PETER 1:6–7 SKJV

Notice that there is a "heaviness" to the trials we go through. (The Bible is always honest about things like that.) But our faith grows stronger as the refining process burns away things like our own self-confidence, the love of money, harsh judgment of others, and assumptions about "the way things ought to be." Your life really isn't about you—it's about God and what He wants to do in and through you.

Don't resist the refining.

"But He knows the way that I take. When He has tested me, I shall come forth as gold."
JOB 23:10 SKJV

May I count it joy, Lord, when You test my faith.
Help me to see what You're trying to accomplish in my life.

45 According to US government statistics, thirty-two people die every day in alcohol-related traffic crashes. Averaged out, that's a death every forty-five minutes.

You sure don't get that perspective from the beer commercials.

Everyone in Partyland, USA, is good-looking, having a blast, and seemingly oblivious to any danger. But there *are* dangers to drinking, and they can be truly life altering—for yourself and for others around you. So to avoid regrets,

DO THIS

Beware of Alcohol

It's true that Jesus, in His first public miracle, changed water into wine (John 2:1–11). And it's true that the apostle Paul told his young assistant Timothy to "use a little wine for your stomach's sake" (1 Timothy 5:23 skjv). But it's also true that God's Word warns about intoxicating drinks over and over again:

Wine is a mocker; strong drink is raging, and whoever is deceived by it is not wise. Proverbs 20:1 skjv

Who has woe? Who has sorrow? Who has contentions? Who has babbling? Who has wounds without cause? Who has redness of eyes? Those who linger long at the wine, those who go to seek mixed wine. Proverbs 23:29–30 skjv

Woe to those who rise up early in the morning, that they may pursue strong drink, who continue until night until wine inflames them! Isaiah 5:11 skjv

Drunkards. . .shall [not] inherit the kingdom of God. 1 Corinthians 6:10 skjv

There are plenty of other verses like these, in addition to stories of the trouble that alcohol caused—such as Noah's embarrassment after the flood (Genesis 9:18–29). God's law prohibited Israel's priests from drinking anything fermented before they served in the tabernacle, on penalty of death (Leviticus 10:9). And then we have John the Baptist's example, as explained by the angel Gabriel:

> *"He shall be great in the sight of the Lord, and shall drink neither wine nor strong drink. And he shall be filled with the Holy Spirit, even from his mother's womb."* LUKE 1:15 SKJV

AVOIDING ALCOHOL WAS PART OF THE OLD TESTAMENT'S "NAZIRITE VOW" (NUMBERS 6).

Does God approve of drunkenness? Clearly He does not. Has He forbidden every use of alcohol? Maybe not—but always remember that teens are bound by the age limits of state and national laws. Is it *wise* to drink? Well, think of it this way: if you never take the first drink, you'll never become drunk. . .you'll never crash a car while intoxicated. . .you'll never become an alcoholic.

That seems like a pretty effective way to banish regret.

> ***Do not be drunk with wine, in which is excess, but be filled with the Spirit.***
> EPHESIANS 5:18 SKJV

Lord, this world loves alcohol, and it's pushing me all the time to join in. Please give me the strength to say no to temptation. Fill me with Your Spirit instead.

46 Theater productions are nothing new. The ancient Greeks were putting on plays hundreds of years before Jesus was born in Bethlehem.

But even the most gung-ho promoter of ancient Greek drama would be stunned at the ubiquity (that is, the "everywhereness") of today's entertainment. You can watch live plays, concerts, sporting events—every kind of program imaginable—in venues everywhere. And from your phone or device or laptop, you can plug into literally millions of movies, TV shows, songs, and funny cat/dog/baby/skateboard accident videos.

Your entertainment options are virtually endless. . .and potentially deadening to your spirit. To avoid serious regret,

DON'T DO THIS
Drown Out God's Voice

Has a parent or teacher ever scolded you for wearing earbuds when they were trying to talk to you? Has a friend ever gotten angry because you were more interested in your screen than him?

Think how God must feel when our entertainments—by definition, much lesser things—take our attention away from Him. With so much noise in our ears, we can miss hearing His voice. With so many images before our eyes, we can overlook the splendors of His Word. In frustration, God may say to us what He said to the disobedient, disrespectful Old Testament Israelites:

> "Hear me, my people, and I will warn you—if you would only listen to me, Israel!" PSALM 81:8 NIV

It's easy to be distracted by all the fun stuff available to us. But "fun stuff" isn't always the best stuff—in fact, it's rarely so. When distraction becomes habit, we might find ourselves less and less interested in God and His Word. . .and that's a very dangerous place to be.

> *"But my people would not listen to me; Israel would not submit to me. So I gave them over to their stubborn hearts to follow their own devices."* PSALM 81:11–12 NIV

NOT COMPUTER DEVICES—BUT AN INTERESTING COINCIDENCE IN TERMS, DON'T YOU THINK?

Of course, our electronics are only one thing that can drown out God's voice in our lives. *Anything* can become a distraction, from girls to sports to cars to jobs to girls. (Did we already say "girls"?) Take this as a friendly warning—beware of anything that consumes your time and energy, leaving you with less for God.

He's always calling to you. Just be sure you're listening for His voice.

> *"Here I am! I stand at the door and knock. If anyone hears my voice and opens the door, I will come in and eat with that person, and they with me."*
> REVELATION 3:20 NIV

Lord, entertainment is easy—listening for Your voice is hard. But hard things make me better. Please give me the desire and the will to spend time in Your Word and prayer. Help me to listen as You speak to me.

47 You know about analogies, right? That's when you make a comparison between two different things because of similarities in certain aspects of each.

Analogies between spiritual things and the world we live in are never perfect. But they can be helpful when they allow us to see things from a new angle.

Here's one: being a Christian is kind of like having your driver's license. There are great privileges to each. There are also some dangers if we misuse our privilege. On that narrow road to a no-regrets life, here's something to remember:

DO THIS

Follow the Rules

As a teenage driver, you have important choices to make: Will you obey speed limits, stop at red lights, stay right of the centerline? These are the rules of the road, and they're basically up to you. If you disobey them, you'll probably find trouble. You might be ticketed—or you could even kill yourself.

The Christian life has "rules of the road" too. All of the Bible's commands tell us about God by showing us what He likes and what He hates. If we disobey, there will be consequences—big or small, now or later. But when we live our lives appropriately, God is pleased.

> *Whoever looks intently into the perfect law that gives freedom, and continues in it—not forgetting what they have heard, but doing it—they will be blessed in what they do.* JAMES 1:25 NIV

Reminder: We don't obey God's laws to be saved. That comes from believing in the one man—Jesus—who did follow the rules perfectly then died on a cross as the sacrifice for sin. But having accepted Christ, having been adopted into God's family by our faith in Jesus, we then need to follow the rules our Father sets. As Creator of all things, He has the right to require obedience.

Jesus, the Son of God who actually is God (part of that mysterious Trinity we've discussed), once said,

> *"You are my friends if you do what I command."* JOHN 15:14 NIV

JESUS SAID THIS RIGHT AFTER SAYING HE WOULD LAY DOWN HIS LIFE FOR HIS FRIENDS.

Moral laws—like those against idolatry, stealing, adultery, and murder—appear in the Old Testament, are repeated in the New, and still apply to us today. Some rules that were specific to the ancient Israelites—relating to food and clothing and sacrifices—are no longer in effect for us (the book of Hebrews really makes this point). Your job is to study God's Word, see what He wants from you today, and do it. You will never regret that pursuit.

The law of the LORD is perfect, refreshing the soul. The statutes of the LORD are trustworthy, making wise the simple.
PSALM 19:7 NIV

Lord Jesus, I can enjoy the benefit of the perfect rule following You did. Now please help me to obey Your rules too, so that You and Your Father will be honored.

48

So what did you think of all that rules talk in the preceding entry?

Some people, by nature, are rebels—they hate being restricted by laws and other people's expectations. But even the rule followers among us will sometimes feel like bucking authority. That goes all the way back to Adam and Eve in the garden of Eden.

Wherever you fall on that spectrum, here's a little encouragement: in your pursuit of a no-regrets life,

DON'T DO THIS

Follow the Rules

Huh?

Yes, that seems to contradict the previous entry. So let me explain: Always follow *God's* rules. Never follow human rules that contradict God's rules.

Ever hear of Shiphrah and Puah? They were midwives—women who helped pregnant women give birth—when the ancient Israelites lived in Egypt. As God's people grew in number, the pharaoh got nervous. He wanted to thin out the Israelite herd, so he told the midwives they could care only for infant girls. . .the boys should be killed. Shiphrah and Puah quietly disobeyed.

> *Because the midwives feared God, they refused to obey the king's orders. They allowed the boys to live, too.* EXODUS 1:17 NLT

The midwives' disobedience to Pharaoh was really obedience to God, and He rewarded them for it (Exodus 1:20–21).

Many centuries later, the prophet Daniel faced a similar dilemma: Should he obey the Persian ruler Darius' silly order that people should pray only to him for the next thirty days? Well, it wasn't really a dilemma, because Daniel had no hesitation in disobeying—and publicly.

> *When Daniel learned that the law had been signed, he went home and knelt down as usual in his upstairs room, with its windows open toward Jerusalem. He prayed three times a day, just as he had always done, giving thanks to his God.*
> DANIEL 6:10 NLT

BRAVE AS HIS FRIENDS SHADRACH, MESHACH, AND ABEDNEGO (DANIEL 3)

Daniel's disobedience—unlike the midwives'—resulted in punishment. But even then, God protected him from the dangers of the lions' den.

Anytime you choose to disobey your government, or even to go against culture, you'll likely pay a price. But can you imagine the regret of the midwives if they had actually killed the baby boys? Or Daniel's regret had he dishonored his God?

That's a very poor trade. When any human rule contradicts God's, you know which one to follow.

> *They called the apostles back in and commanded them never again to speak or teach in the name of Jesus. But Peter and John replied, "Do you think God wants us to obey you rather than him? We cannot stop telling about everything we have seen and heard."*
> ACTS 4:18–20 NLT

Lord, I'll need wisdom to know if and when I should disobey human rules and expectations—and then the courage to follow through. Please guide me by Your Spirit, helping me always to honor You.

49 Are you aware of special days throughout the year that recognize women? Mother's Day (the second Sunday of May) is well known. But there are also Grandma's Day (January 21), the International Day of Women and Girls in Science (February 11), National Women in Agriculture Day (March 24), and Women Veterans Day (June 12), to name some others.

You might be thinking, *Why are we talking about women's days in a book for teen guys?* Good question!

Women are arguably God's greatest creation. Consider: He made Adam on the last day of creation week. . .but His ultimate act was making *Eve* to complete Adam. Sadly, throughout history many men have mistreated women. Let's never do that—and avoid the regret that inevitably follows for a Christian guy.

DO THIS

Honor Women

As always, Jesus set the perfect example. In a culture dismissive of women, He welcomed them as followers—think of the sisters Mary and Martha, and His good friend Mary Magdalene. She, along with ladies named Joanna and Susanna, actually helped to fund Jesus' ministry (see Luke 8:1–3).

Then there was Jesus' interaction with "the woman at the well" of Sychar, in the "enemy territory" of Samaria. He already knew about her five marriages and the fact that she was now just living with someone. But Jesus looked past those things and the Jewish people's cultural roadblocks:

> When a Samaritan woman came to draw water, Jesus said to her, "Will you give me a drink?" . . . The Samaritan woman said to him, "You are a Jew and I am a Samaritan woman.

How can you ask me for a drink?" (For Jews do not associate with Samaritans.) John 4:7, 9 NIV

ASKING QUESTIONS IS A GREAT WAY TO APPROACH PEOPLE.

She became a believer that day—something God wants for every man, woman, boy, and girl (2 Peter 3:9).

You can help the cause by treating every woman respectfully. Start with your mom. Follow up with teachers, neighbors, any lady you meet. By all means, treat the girls you date respectfully. God can use the honor you show to point people to Jesus, who welcomes all.

In Christ Jesus you are all children of God through faith, for all of you who were baptized into Christ have clothed yourselves with Christ. There is neither Jew nor Gentile, neither slave nor free, nor is there male and female, for you are all one in Christ Jesus. Galatians 3:26–28 NIV

Does that mean we're all exactly the same? Of course not. Jesus taught that God made us "male and female" (Matthew 19:4 NIV), and we all have different passions, abilities, and physical characteristics. Those differences, you know, make women *really* interesting.

**Charm is deceptive, and beauty is fleeting; but a
woman who fears the Lord is to be praised.**
Proverbs 31:30 NIV

*Lord Jesus, give me Your love for all people,
and help me to treat women with complete
respect. I want to point everyone to You.*

50 Teen guys = cool. You've been paying your dues, and now you rule the school—or you're about to. You know how to dress. You've got the language down. You might even have your driver's license.

Okay, you're probably still trying to figure out girls. But you *know* that you're way past those silly elementary school kids. The crazy TV shows they watch! The goofy toys they like! Their ignorance of pretty much everything! Now that you're a teen, you're done with *kids*.

Hopefully, that's an exaggeration. But little kids can try your patience. They might interfere with your plans or get into your stuff. They can be a pain. . .and also a blast. Don't disregard them. To avoid regret,

DO THIS
Respect Children

You know, you're not so far removed from childhood yourself. Not too long ago, your mom or dad, aunts and uncles, teachers and coaches were putting up with *your* silliness. Maybe even a teen brother or guy from church gave you his time. Wasn't it great to have their attention?

Jesus wasn't "too important" for little kids. He was almost always surrounded by people—His twelve disciples and huge crowds that needed healing and teaching. When people brought their little kids to see Him, the disciples—thinking they were helping—tried to shoo them away. How did Jesus respond?

He was very displeased and said to them, "Allow the little children to come to Me, and do not forbid them, for of such is the kingdom of God. Truly I say to you, whoever shall not

receive the kingdom of God as a little child, he shall not enter in it." And He took them up in His arms, put His hands on them, and blessed them. MARK 10:14–16 SKJV

SEE WHAT MAKES JESUS "VERY DISPLEASED"!

Little kids are open, honest, trusting—exactly how we should be as we come to Jesus. We can learn from them, if we're not too "cool."

Sure, kids have some growing up to do. That's the way life works. But even the very young can play important roles in God's plan. Remember when the Lord called young Samuel at night, telling him what would happen to the priest Eli and his sons (1 Samuel 3)? God was already developing the prophet who would ultimately lead Israel.

The child Samuel grew on and was in favor both with the LORD and also with men. 1 SAMUEL 2:26 SKJV

Think about this: maybe *you* could influence a child who is destined for significance. When little Liam or Owen or Declan wants your attention, smile and share what older people have shared with you. That reflects the God who loves children.

Like a shepherd, [God] shall feed His flock. He shall gather the lambs with His arm and carry them in His bosom.
ISAIAH 40:11 SKJV

Keep me humble, Lord, ready to engage with whoever You bring into my life.

51 If there were an Olympic medal for being offended, millions of highly qualified competitors would jostle for the award. Of course, as soon as the honor had been bestowed on the single most offended person in the world, everyone else would be even more offended than when they began.

These days, it seems like people everywhere are looking for reasons to be ticked off. You'll find the offended on talk shows and in political debates, scuffling on playing fields and committing acts of road rage. If you're a Christian (and I truly hope that's the case), here's a good way to avoid regrets in both the short and long term:

DON'T DO THIS
Take Offense

Is everyone in this world nice? No, of course not. Are they often oblivious to you and your interests? Yes, absolutely. Does it help to get mad and lash out at them? We'll let you answer that question.

Here is God's perspective on taking offense, some Holy Spirit–inspired truth written down by the once-very-wise-but-then-threw-it-all-away-and-then-came-around-again-to-sanity-late-in-life King Solomon:

> *Patience is better than pride. Do not be quickly provoked in your spirit, for anger resides in the lap of fools.* ECCLESIASTES 7:8–9 NIV

A young couple, making their first flight with their one-year-old daughter, got to the airport late. (That happens when young kids are in the family equation.) The harried gate agent snapped, "You've missed your plane!" Rather than respond in kind, the dad said apologetically, "Oh, wow. . .what can we do about that?"

That mild answer worked a kind of magic. The airline employee immediately calmed down and got to work changing the family's tickets. They ultimately reached their destination even sooner than they'd planned.

Responding gently doesn't guarantee that things will go your way. But when you allow the Holy Spirit to drive your actions and reactions—when you don't take offense at every provocation—you're reflecting God Himself. And that's always a good thing.

> *For this very reason, make every effort to add to your faith goodness; and to goodness, knowledge; and to knowledge, self-control; and to self-control, perseverance; and to perseverance, godliness; and to godliness, mutual affection; and to mutual affection, love.* 2 Peter 1:5–7 NIV

LOOK UP VERSES 3 AND 4 TO UNDERSTAND THAT "FOR THIS VERY REASON" PHRASE.

Angry, insulting, even physically aggressive reactions are a serious problem in our world. Choose to respond differently. You'll never regret keeping the gas can away from the fire.

> *A person's wisdom yields patience; it is to one's glory to overlook an offense.*
> Proverbs 19:11 NIV

I'll need Your help, Lord, to respond gently to other people. Sometimes they're so annoying. . .but I guess I can be too. Please work in my life to make me more like Jesus.

52 Be honest: Have you ever seen unsaved people living it up and thought, *Why can't I have fun like that?*

Many—if not most—Christians have felt this inner tug-of-war. We try to play by the rules, but it seems like cheaters are the ones who get ahead. They make the money, buy the toys, win the girls. As you get older, your frustrations might even grow—the people who don't follow God often seem healthier, happier, less troubled than those who deny themselves and sacrifice for others. Even believers can begin to wonder, *Is the Christian life really worth it?*

Spoiler alert: yes, of course. On the way to the explanation, we'll consider this rule for a no-regrets life:

DON'T DO THIS

Envy Sinners

You recall that we said this frustration isn't unusual? Even a psalm writer—a Bible author!—wrestled with it. After saying, "Truly God is good to Israel, to those whose hearts are pure" (Psalm 73:1 NLT), Asaph admitted,

> But as for me, I almost lost my footing. My feet were slipping, and I was almost gone. For I envied the proud when I saw them prosper despite their wickedness. PSALM 73:2–3 NLT

One danger of envying sinners is that we'll be tempted to do what they do. We might look for an escape from our disappointments through alcohol or drugs or sex or spending or any number of troublesome pursuits—all centering on basic selfishness. But here's why living life as a God-honoring, Bible-believing, Jesus-loving, others-focused Christian is indeed worth it:

> *So I tried to understand why the wicked prosper. But what a difficult task it is! Then I went into your sanctuary, O God, and I finally understood the destiny of the wicked.* Psalm 73:16–17 NLT

THIS IS HEAVY STUFF....

Asaph the psalm writer finally recognized something Jesus explained centuries later. Jesus described a poor, sick beggar named Lazarus, who lay outside the gate of a rich man's house, longing for a scrap or two from his feasts. The rich man ignored Lazarus—the only attention the poor guy got was from the neighborhood dogs, which licked his open sores.

But things changed dramatically when each man died. Faithful Lazarus went to his eternal reward, while the selfish rich man was punished. In Jesus' story, the Old Testament hero Abraham told the rich man, "Son, remember that during your lifetime you had everything you wanted, and Lazarus had nothing. So now he is here being comforted, and you are in anguish" (Luke 16:25 NLT).

When you feel like *you* have nothing in this world, stay faithful to God. He'll make sure you are well rewarded in the end.

Don't envy sinners, but always continue to fear the LORD.
Proverbs 23:17 NLT

It's hard to be content, Lord, but I know that's what You call me to do. Please give me Your long view of life—the eternal view—to keep me faithful here.

53 Wouldn't it be cool if your name went down in history?

Ever heard of the Geiger counter? That radiation-detection device was named for its German inventor, Hans Geiger. How about the Fosbury flop? The technique that changed high jumping was named for American Olympian Dick Fosbury. Maybe you've read a Kafkaesque story—one that's strangely complex or illogical—named for Czech author Franz Kafka.

Then there are ways you *don't* want to be remembered. Revolutionary war general Benedict Arnold is known as a Quisling (another person's name, meaning "traitor"). An American commander, Arnold conspired with the British in what one founding father called "the blackest treason."

Scholars still debate Arnold's motives, but one thing is clear: he's the biggest betrayer in American history. To avoid the regret of that kind of legacy,

DO THIS

Live with Integrity

Integrity is strong adherence to a moral code—and we Christians know that code is God's. In a word, integrity is *incorruptibility*. No amount of aggravation, mockery, or money can separate you from the commitments you've made to God and others. Whatever pressures come, you hold to what you know is right. An average soldier in Old Testament times set a great example.

King David's son Absalom was trying to steal his father's throne, but the loving dad urged his soldiers to treat the young man gently. In a battle in a woods, Absalom got his beautiful long hair snarled in a low-hanging tree limb. When a soldier told his commander what he'd seen, Joab bellowed, "Why didn't you strike him to the ground right there? Then I would have had to give you ten shekels of silver and a warrior's belt" (2 Samuel 18:11 NIV). The unnamed warrior's response is golden:

> *"Even if a thousand shekels were weighed out into my hands, I would not lay a hand on the king's son."* 2 SAMUEL 18:12 NIV

WHAT'S RIGHT IS PRICELESS.

A lot of people give up their integrity for money. Some do so over frustration with the way they've been treated. These days, many say things they don't believe or apologize for things they do believe, tossing their integrity in hopes of keeping the peace. This is no way for a Christian to live.

> *The integrity of the upright guides them, but the unfaithful are destroyed by their duplicity.* PROVERBS 11:3 NIV

We need to read the Bible in ultimate terms, with a long-range view of what's being said. Does duplicity destroy the unfaithful immediately? No. . .many of them succeed wildly in this world. But don't overlook the words *in this world*. Unless they change their ways and truly follow Jesus, unfaithful people will certainly be destroyed.

Be the upright guy, the man of integrity. You'll receive God's guidance through this life and into eternity.

And there's no regret in that.

> *Because of my integrity you uphold me and set me in your presence forever.*
> PSALM 41:12 NIV

I want a good name, Lord. Help me to live with integrity.

54 There's always *that* guy.

In preschool or the church nursery, someone is hoarding all the toys. "Sharing" is a foreign concept to him. In the older grades, someone is vacuuming up pizza and cookies at the class party or youth group event. "Restraint" is a foreign concept to him. In adult life, someone is lying, cheating, stealing, and otherwise steamrolling his peers in pursuit of money, opportunities, women, you name it. "Contentment" is a foreign concept to him.

It's not a pretty sight.

We hate being around takers, but let's be honest—it's a temptation that hits us all at one time or another. Here's an important signpost on the path to a no-regrets life:

DON'T DO THIS
Be Greedy

We all need things—like that well-known trio of "food, clothing, and shelter"—and the apostle Paul promised, "My God will meet all your needs" (Philippians 4:19 NIV). But never confuse *needs* with *wants*. Yes, you need a house to live in—no, you don't need a twenty-million-dollar Malibu mansion. You do need transportation—but you don't need a fleet of Italian sports cars. Sometimes a basic peanut butter sandwich is better for you than a giant buffet.

What would Jesus think about this? We know *exactly* what He thinks:

> *"Watch out! Be on your guard against all kinds of greed; life does not consist in an abundance of possessions."* LUKE 12:15 NIV

Greed makes people do stupid, crazy, even dangerous things—things that cause regret for all involved. Closely related to "coveting," greed can take us beyond wanting physical stuff to a desire even to possess people. The last of the Ten Commandments indicates where so many of our problems come from:

> "You shall not covet your neighbor's house. You shall not covet your neighbor's wife, or his male or female servant, his ox or donkey, or anything that belongs to your neighbor."
> EXODUS 20:17 NIV

TEN-COMMANDMENT TROUBLES—LYING, STEALING,
ADULTERY, MURDER—ALL START RIGHT HERE.

As a Christian teen, ask God to help you find the right balance in life: you need to have goals and work toward a successful career, but you don't ever want to cross the line into a destructive greediness. This is a matter for serious prayer. Don't let yourself become *that* guy.

Since, then, you have been raised with Christ, set your hearts on things above, where Christ is, seated at the right hand of God. Set your minds on things above, not on earthly things. . . . Put to death, therefore, whatever belongs to your earthly nature: sexual immorality, impurity, lust, evil desires and greed, which is idolatry.
COLOSSIANS 3:1–2, 5 NIV

*Lord, I want to stand apart from this greedy world.
Help me to be content, trusting You for everything I need.*

55 We swim in a sea of "experts," many of them predicting terrible things if we don't follow their wise advice. But how good can their ideas be when they change so often?

Last year, doctors said a certain food was bad for you—this year they announce it's actually healthy. Environmentalists were saying we had only ten years to disaster *thirty* years ago. Financial wizards say you should put your money into tech stocks. . .no, cryptocurrency. . .no, gold! It's really kind of exhausting.

If you let it, all of this back-and-forth will make you crazy. Too much attention to what people say—and not enough to the solid, unchanging truths of God—will definitely lead to regret (and very possibly a permanent migraine). So then,

DO THIS

Question Man, Trust God

Sure, some people have a lot more training and experience than the rest of us, and we should respect that. But a doctor or a teacher or a scientist or even a pastor can be wrong—so whatever anyone tells us should be compared against the truth we find in the Bible. In the first-century church at Berea—now Veria, Greece—Christians even checked up on the apostle Paul:

> *These were more noble than those in Thessalonica, in that they received the word with all readiness of mind and searched the scriptures daily to see whether these things were so.* ACTS 17:11 SKJV

THESE PEOPLE WERE CALLED "NOBLE" FOR DOUBLE-CHECKING AN APOSTLE!

Of course, God's Word doesn't speak specifically to every issue we face today. But its principles do. Regarding your health, the fear of the Lord is good for you (Proverbs 3:7–8). About the environment? God will protect this earth until *He's* done with it (Genesis 8:21–22). About money and finances? "God shall supply all your need according to His riches in glory by Christ Jesus" (Philippians 4:19 SKJV). There's no need for worry (see Luke 12:22–28). Always trust God.

And always *obey* God, especially when man says otherwise. Shortly after Jesus returned to heaven and sent down His Spirit to live in believers, the church was booming. Jewish leaders hated that and tried to muzzle the apostles, forbidding them to teach in the Lord's name. Their response?

> *Peter and the other apostles answered and said, "We ought to obey God rather than men." ACTS 5:29 SKJV*

No man (or woman) should ever come between you and God. To avoid regrets, question everything you hear from human lips. Test it against God's Word.

> *Whoever looks into the perfect law of liberty and continues in it—not being a forgetful hearer but a doer of the work—this man shall be blessed in his deed.*
> JAMES 1:25 SKJV

So many people want to tell me what to do, Lord— but You alone are truth. Lead me deep into Your Word so I can live with confidence. I want to trust You!

56 Don't you hate being misunderstood? Especially if the other person simply isn't listening to you?

Sometimes you want to scream, "That's not what I mean! You're not picking up what I'm laying down! Just pay attention!"

Ever stop to think that *God* might feel that way too? He created an incredible universe that points directly to Him, but many people come up with elaborate (and, honestly, *silly*) ideas to explain Him away. He provided an actual record of His ways and thoughts and desires (the Bible, of course), but it's hated and mocked by millions.

Hopefully, you're not part of that crowd. But there's a danger even for those of us who believe in God and follow Him through faith in Jesus: sometimes, by carelessness and ignorance, we don't know and follow His Word as we should.

Here's an important rule for avoiding regret in this life:

DON'T DO THIS

Assume and Presume

It's easy—even for church-attending Christians—to think we know what God wants when we're really chasing our own desires. Have you ever heard anyone say (or even thought to yourself), "God wants me to be happy"? No verse in the Bible specifically says that, and if happiness means "I can do whatever I please," then the idea is 100 percent false. But you have to spend some real time and thought on God's Word to understand why.

The truth is there for you, if you choose to pursue it.

> "I am the LORD, and there is no other. I have not spoken in secret, from somewhere in a land of darkness; I have not said to Jacob's descendants, 'Seek me in vain.' " ISAIAH 45:18–19 NIV

TRUE FOR ANCIENT ISRAEL, TRUE FOR US TODAY

Just for a moment, let's get back to that idea of happiness. In reality, God wants you to be *good*—trusting Him, obeying His Word, living like Jesus—which leads to joy (a "fruit of the Spirit," from Galatians 5:22–23). Joy carries you through the inevitable hardships of life. But joy comes on God's terms, not yours.

When we *assume* we know God's will without knowing His Word, we *presume* on Him. And that can be a dangerous thing.

> "A prophet who presumes to speak in my name anything I have not commanded, or a prophet who speaks in the name of other gods, is to be put to death." DEUTERONOMY 18:20 NIV

We can never know everything about God. But we can certainly know everything we *need* to know about Him. It's in His Word. Read it and heed it—don't assume and presume.

Show me your ways, LORD, teach me your paths. Guide me in your truth and teach me, for you are God my Savior.
PSALM 25:4–5 NIV

Open my heart to Your will, Lord. It's so easy to think I know everything—but that's Your specialty. Make me humble and ready to learn.

57 Don't take everything too seriously. A little dent in your fender might be frustrating, but it won't change your life. Getting turned down for a date isn't the end of the world—millions of guys have experienced that, and the earth still spins on its axis. Your favorite pro team missed the playoffs? There are certainly better ways to spend your emotional capital than fussing over cocky young multimillionaires.

Don't even take yourself too seriously, okay? We all make plenty of embarrassing mistakes in life. Learn to laugh things off and keep moving forward.

But one thing is worth every ounce of care and concern you can muster. To avoid the biggest, deepest, most depressing regret of all,

DO THIS

Take Sin Seriously

Sin is as much a part of your genetic makeup as your XY chromosomes. Somehow, Adam and Eve's disobedience has messed up every person since that time. (Well, except Jesus.) The first couple's failure has caused havoc in humanity.

None of us could avoid our sin nature, but we all have to admit that we've made full use of it—making selfish and destructive choices that dishonor God. And there's a heavy consequence for that:

> *You get what is coming to you when you sin. It is death!*
> ROMANS 6:23 NLV

KEEP READING FOR THE GOOD NEWS....

You may already know there's a much happier second half to Romans 6:23 (NLV): "But God's free gift is life that lasts forever. It is given to us by our Lord Jesus Christ."

Gifts are great, but they have to be accepted. Imagine that someone offers you a check for ten million dollars. If you say, "Cool" but don't actually receive the check, it won't do you any good at all.

Salvation is a lot like that. Eternal life through Jesus is free for the taking—so make very sure you've humbly received it by faith.

> God was so good to make a way for us to be saved from the punishment of sin. What makes us think we will not go to hell if we do not take the way to heaven that He has made for us? HEBREWS 2:3 NLV

This is by far the most important issue in life. Your eternal destiny depends on what you do about sin—but there's no amount of self-sacrifice that can cover your debt to God. *Jesus* was the sacrifice, and all He wants is your faith in Him. Have you accepted His gift?

> *If you say with your mouth that Jesus is Lord, and believe in your heart that God raised Him from the dead, you will be saved from the punishment of sin.*
> ROMANS 10:9 NLV

Thank You, Lord Jesus, for paying the price for my sin. I believe that God the Father raised You from the dead to prove Your power over death. I want to live for You, now and forever.

58 If you take Guinness World Records as the authority, the award for the longest marriage goes to David and Sarah Hiller. The couple spoke their vows on April 23, 1809, in Jamestown, Canada—and kept them for nearly eighty-nine years until Mrs. Hiller's death on April 8, 1898. David and Sarah were nineteen and seventeen, respectively, when they married.

You sometimes hear of "childhood sweethearts" who marry young and stand the test of time. But a lot of times, our teen crushes dry up like Play-Doh on a hot sidewalk. We can't avoid the emotional fireworks that go off inside us, but to steer clear of regrets,

DON'T DO THIS
Rush into Serious Relationships

Yes, a few guys will end up with their teenage crush for life. But odds are you'll settle down with someone you meet later, after you've had time to mature. Either way, love is natural, something that God both hard-wires and programs into you. And that goes back to the very beginning, to the creation week of Genesis:

> The LORD God said, "It is not good for the man to be alone. I will make a helper suitable for him." GENESIS 2:18 NIV

In our world—unlike in Bible times—young people typically date. You seek out a girl who interests you; then you try to interest her. If that goes well, you become boyfriend and girlfriend and stop dating other people. (Unless you're a real skunk.)

Dating is a great opportunity to learn more about yourself, your girl, and relationships in general. And when you're still in your teens, there's a lot to be learned. That's why you'll do well not to rush things. Certainly sex, since God is clear that sex is limited to marriage (Exodus 20:14; Matthew 5:28; 1 Corinthians 7:1–2; Ephesians 5:3; and we could go on), but also just an emotional attachment you might not be ready for.

Here is God's standard for a guy committing to a woman:

> *Husbands, love your wives, just as Christ loved the church and gave himself up for her to make her holy, cleansing her by the washing with water through the word, and to present her to himself as a radiant church, without stain or wrinkle or any other blemish, but holy and blameless. In this same way, husbands ought to love their wives as their own bodies.*
> EPHESIANS 5:25–28 NIV

IT'S A VERY HIGH STANDARD.

If you're not quite ready for that level of self-sacrifice, that's okay. Better to recognize that now than to rush into some serious relationship that may not turn out well. Give yourself—and God— time. There's no need to rush.

As servants of God we commend ourselves in every way. . .in purity, understanding, patience and kindness.
2 CORINTHIANS 6:4, 6 NIV

Lead me, Lord God, into the right relationship at the right time. I want to follow Your rules and Your guidance so that my future marriage is great.

59 Can you worship God in nature? Sure. The rolling surf of the ocean, the soaring majesty of the mountains, the millions of stars in the expanse of the night sky—they all can point you to the astounding Creator who spoke everything into existence. If you're an outdoorsy type, make sure you acknowledge God when you're enjoying His handiwork.

Can you worship God in nature as well as you can in church? Probably not.

Why? Because God created His people for relationships. He intended them to live and work and worship in community. And that community, in this twenty-first century after Jesus walked the earth, is the church.

So for a no-regrets life, here's an important rule:

DON'T DO THIS
Skip Church

Yes, you're busy. We get that. And getting up each Sunday morning for church is just another thing on your to-do list. Well, not really.

Attending church is something to do, but it's much more than a job or a game with your travel team. Church is where you worship the God of the universe, the all-powerful, all-knowing, all-loving Lord who gives you the ability to work or play sports. Church is also a place to find challenge and encouragement from your fellow Christians. That has always been important, but in these times we're living in, it's absolutely essential.

> *Let us think of ways to motivate one another to acts of love and good works. And let us not neglect our meeting together, as some people do, but encourage one another, especially now that the day of his return is drawing near.* HEBREWS 10:24–25 NLT

When Hebrews mentions "the day of his return," it means Jesus' return, His second coming to earth to reward His followers and set everything right. To be ready and eager for that day, you'll need all the help you can get from your church—good Bible preaching, inspiring worship, the kind of personal interactions that push you to greater love for God and service to His people.

If you're still not convinced of the importance of church attendance, here's the example of Jesus Himself:

> *When he came to the village of Nazareth, his boyhood home, he went as usual to the synagogue on the Sabbath.* LUKE 4:16 NLT

"AS USUAL"—IT WAS JESUS' HABIT.

When you first believed in Jesus, accepting Him as your Savior and Lord, you became part of His "body" (Colossians 1:18)—what many call the "universal church." But Jesus' universal body is made up of local church bodies, where people learn and serve and grow together.

You don't want to miss that.

I was glad when they said to me, "Let us go to the house of the LORD."
PSALM 122:1 NLT

Thank You, Lord, for the church. Please help me to make it a priority in my life. I need all the support and encouragement I can get!

60 Ever said to yourself, "Man, I wish someone would. . ."?

Maybe there's trash lying around your school: "Man, I wish someone would pick that up." Maybe there's a scraggly cat roaming your neighborhood: "Man, I wish someone would take care of that thing." Maybe there's a need for umpires in the youth baseball league: "Man, I wish someone would volunteer to help."

Someone might say to you, "*You're* someone."

Perhaps you're the person who's needed to accomplish good things in your family, your school, your community. And don't forget that other important place where God's kids meet each week. We can mumble and complain about what's not being done, or—to make things better and head off regrets—we can

DO THIS

Serve at Church

The Bible talks a lot about "spiritual gifts," those special skills and abilities that God gives His children specifically for service. Check out this list from the book of Romans:

> Just as each of us has one body with many members, and these members do not all have the same function, so in Christ we, though many, form one body, and each member belongs to all the others. We have different gifts, according to the grace given to each of us. If your gift is prophesying, then prophesy in accordance with your faith; if it is serving, then serve; if it is teaching, then teach; if it is to encourage, then give encouragement; if it is giving, then give generously; if it is to lead, do it diligently; if it is to show mercy, do it cheerfully. ROMANS 12:4–8 NIV

UP FRONT OR IN THE BACKGROUND, THERE'S A PLACE FOR YOU.

Some people have a special calling to make the ministry their job. But those of us who aren't paid pastors or youth leaders or worship team members should still find slots that suit our talents and serve others. Maybe you could help with Vacation Bible School or children's church. . .maybe the audiovisual team could use volunteers. . .maybe you could visit the older church members who don't get out like they used to. . .maybe you could do whatever "I wish someone would."

> Let's not get tired of doing what is good. At just the right time we will reap a harvest of blessing if we don't give up. Therefore, whenever we have the opportunity, we should do good to everyone—especially to those in the family of faith.
> GALATIANS 6:9–10 NLT

You're someone. Your church needs you. You'll never regret getting involved and serving your fellow Christians.

> *Love each other with genuine affection, and take delight in honoring each other. Never be lazy, but work hard and serve the Lord enthusiastically.*
> ROMANS 12:10–11 NLT

Show me where You want me to serve, Lord, and then help me to do it well. May I never say, "I wish someone would" when I'm the one who can.

61 The basic message of the Bible is simple: God made you, loves you, and wants you in His family. As you learn more about the Bible, you build on that foundation. You realize that God is a trinity of Father, Son, and Spirit. You see that the Son—Jesus—died on a cross to pay the sin debt separating every human being from God. When you put your faith in Jesus, you are saved from the punishment for sin. God's Spirit lives in you, and you are destined for heaven rather than hell.

That just scratches the surface of who God is and what He wants for you—you could study scripture for a lifetime and still be learning on the day you die. Since the Bible is a big book, full of deep, rich truth, it's so important that you

DON'T DO THIS

Get Your Theology from Memes and T-Shirts

Theology is the study of God and His relationship to the world. He gave us His Word to explain everything we need to know—but He expects us to work at really understanding it. As we apply ourselves, God's Spirit reveals additional truth.

Beware of little sayings about God that have a ring of truth but leave much unsaid. For example, have you ever seen or heard this statement: "Hey, Jesus hung out with prostitutes and sinners"? There is some truth in that, as Jesus—calling Himself "the Son of Man"—proves:

> "John came neither eating nor drinking, and they say, 'He has a demon.' The Son of Man came eating and drinking, and they say, 'Here is a glutton and a drunkard, a friend of tax collectors and sinners.' " MATTHEW 11:18–19 NIV

But if by saying, "Jesus hung out with prostitutes and sinners," someone means that He accepted their sin, that's bad theology. Read other parts of the Bible to see that while Jesus welcomed all people, He never gave them permission to live in sin. Here are snippets of two interactions Jesus had, first with a woman caught in adultery and second with a lame man He'd healed:

> *"Go now and leave your life of sin."* JOHN 8:11 NIV

> *"See, you are well again. Stop sinning or something worse may happen to you."* JOHN 5:14 NIV

GOD'S MORAL LAWS ARE FOR ALL TIME.

The point is simply this: The Bible contains everything God chose to share with humanity. It allows us to know Him and ourselves, to understand sin and salvation. Study it! You'll regret reducing its truth to something that fits on a T-shirt.

"Do not think that I have come to abolish the Law or the Prophets; I have not come to abolish them but to fulfill them."
MATTHEW 5:17 NIV

Lord God, please give me understanding of Your Word. I don't want to be careless and believe the half-truths the world tells.

62 The worst regret of all may be a wasted life.

The person who never finds real purpose just drifts through life—but drifts fast. He's like a guy in a rowboat on the Niagara River, headed for the falls. . .and he doesn't even have oars. He's picking up speed toward the inevitable bad ending.

The ending is happy for those of us who follow Jesus. There will be joy in God's presence forever after we die (Psalm 16:11). But even this life will be happier and more fulfilling if we find the purpose God has for each of us. And we find that purpose when we

DO THIS

Understand Spiritual Gifts

Have you heard that phrase yet? Spiritual gifts are special interests and abilities that the Holy Spirit gives you, at the direction of Jesus:

> *Christ gave gifts to men. He gave to some the gift to be missionaries, some to be preachers, others to be preachers who go from town to town. He gave others the gift to be church leaders and teachers. These gifts help His people work well for Him. And then the church which is the body of Christ will be made strong.* EPHESIANS 4:11–12 NLV

Ephesians 4 lists several gifts that are specific to church workers—pastors, missionaries, evangelists, teachers, and leaders. But there are other passages, like Romans 12 and 1 Corinthians 12, that mention other spiritual gifts for nonprofessional Christians. These are things like encouragement, giving, wisdom, helping, and showing mercy. Every gift is important, every Christian gets at least one, and every time they're used, Jesus' body—the church— becomes stronger.

There are different kinds of gifts. But it is the same Holy Spirit Who gives them. There are different kinds of work to be done for Him. But the work is for the same Lord. There are different ways of doing His work. But it is the same God who uses all these ways in all people. The Holy Spirit works in each person in one way or another for the good of all.
1 CORINTHIANS 12:4–7 NLV

A LOT OF *DIVERSITY* FOR THE GOAL OF *UNITY*

Your gifts will probably align with the talents and interests God has already built into you. But He may also stretch you, challenging you to go beyond what's comfortable so that you really have to trust Him. Ask God for guidance—and maybe talk to your pastor or youth leader too. Once you figure out your gift (or gifts), get to work!

Christ has put each part of the church in its right place. Each part helps other parts. This is what is needed to keep the whole body together. In this way, the whole body grows strong in love.
EPHESIANS 4:16 NLV

What are my gifts, Lord Jesus? Please show me what You want me to do in this life, and then strengthen me to do it well.

63 Throughout much of human history, idols were figurines made of wood, stone, or metal. In modern culture, they tend to be actors, musicians, athletes, and politicians. Sadly, both groups receive the worship that the one true God deserves.

Your mom or grandma or great-grandma might recall their girlfriends swooning over musicians like NSYNC, Michael Jackson, or Elvis Presley. Your dad or grandpa or great-grandpa might remember guys wanting to be like Barack Obama, Harrison Ford, or Mickey Mantle. Respect for another person's capabilities is one thing—but assigning a godlike status to anyone is never a good idea.

Here's some wise guidance for your path to a no-regrets life:

DON'T DO THIS

Idolize Anyone

When God created human beings, He clearly built a desire for worship into our hearts. Of course, that worship should be directed only toward Him. But God knows the way people think, and the temptation we would face to stray from Him—otherwise, why make this the first of the Ten Commandments?

"You shall have no other gods before me." EXODUS 20:3 NIV

Many people who grew up before social media find it strange that "influencers" can have millions of "followers" who hang on their every post. But the social media generation might ask the same question of the old-timers: What made Clark Gable or Marilyn Monroe or John F. Kennedy or Joe Namath or Tiger Woods so special?

Human idols come and go. Sometimes their influence is entirely negative, but you can count on even the most positive, upbeat—

dare we say, *Christian*—celebrity to fail in some way. Every human idol is merely human, you know. That's why we should never put anyone on the proverbial pedestal—even those people who preach and teach God's Word.

> *When one says, "I follow Paul," and another, "I follow Apollos," are you not mere human beings? What, after all, is Apollos? And what is Paul? Only servants, through whom you came to believe—as the Lord has assigned to each his task.* 1 CORINTHIANS 3:4–5 NIV

HUMBLY WRITTEN BY PAUL HIMSELF

Christians know that only one person is worthy of worship: God Himself. And when we overlook the great Creator in favor of people He created, we're just asking for trouble.

But when we honor God above all others, we'll stand out from a world that emphasizes far lesser beings. Don't worry about being "strange" in other people's eyes. The only eyes that matter are God's.

> **This is what the LORD says: "Cursed is the one who trusts in man, who draws strength from mere flesh and whose heart turns away from the LORD."**
> **JEREMIAH 17:5 NIV**

Forgive me, Lord, for the times I've put anyone ahead of You. Help me to truly and faithfully worship You alone.

64 How many ways do we use the word *love*?

Do you love pizza? You probably love your mom or grandma. Maybe you love soccer, Lamborghinis, or Christian rap. Wow, do you love that cute girl in your algebra class. . . .

Of course, we also love dogs, the ocean, action movies, chocolate chip cookies. . .the list is pretty much endless.

But what *is* love, really? That's an important question, and we'll fend off regrets in our lives when we

DO THIS

Define *Love* Accurately

In most of the examples above, we use the word *love* for things we enjoy at one time or another. That cute girl in algebra might be replaced in your thoughts by a cuter girl in English comp. Your love for Lamborghinis might fade over time, superseded by a passion for Porsches.

Your "love" for your mom or grandma gets closer to the real deal. You've known their kindness and gentleness and generosity your whole life, and you want to respond in similar ways (even though we all fail at times). Ideally, the love within a family should be what the Bible describes:

> *Love is patient, love is kind. It does not envy, it does not boast, it is not proud. It does not dishonor others, it is not self-seeking, it is not easily angered, it keeps no record of wrongs. Love does not delight in evil but rejoices with the truth. It always protects, always trusts, always hopes, always perseveres. Love never fails.* 1 CORINTHIANS 13:4–8 NIV

PEOPLE CALL 1 CORINTHIANS 13 THE "LOVE CHAPTER."

That's not a whimsical, here-today-gone-tomorrow kind of "love." What 1 Corinthians 13 lays out is a deep, ongoing commitment to another person's well-being. It's the kind of love God shows to His children, though sadly, they often don't reciprocate.

> *"What can I do with you, Ephraim? What can I do with you, Judah? Your love is like the morning mist, like the early dew that disappears."* Hosea 6:4 NIV

Love like a mist, love that disappears like the morning dew, is just a feeling. Love that lasts is a choice—a firm decision to stick with someone through every circumstance, good, bad, and in between. Real love is what makes marriages and families succeed—not only survive but thrive. It's the commitment we should make to God our Father, who proved His love by sending His Son, Jesus, to die on the cross for our sins.

Now is a great time to commit to real love. It will save you a lot of regret over the course of your life.

God's love has been poured out into our hearts
through the Holy Spirit, who has been given to us.
Romans 5:5 NIV

Heavenly Father, my feelings may say I'm "in love"—but I know that You set the standard of an ongoing commitment that benefits the other person. Help me to love like You do.

65 In the pantheon of great fictional characters, Atticus Finch converses with Frodo Baggins. Sherlock Holmes charms Juliet Capulet. James Bond keeps an eye on Tom Sawyer, who looks to be plotting mischief.

Meanwhile, scuttling around on his little red legs, Mr. Krabs is pop-eyed at the expensive decor of the hall.

What? You don't think SpongeBob SquarePants' boss belongs in this august collection of book and movie characters? C'mon, for pure entertainment value, the great cheapskate of Bikini Bottom never disappoints. Mr. Krabs once had both of his arms ripped off rather than let go of a single dime!

We laugh at a cartoon character who hoards his money, but that's not a great look in real life. Piles of dollars—no matter how big—can never replace real human beings. So to avoid the regret of a well-funded loneliness,

DON'T DO THIS
Be Stingy

All that we have really belongs to God—He created everything, He distributes it as He sees fit, and He expects us to share with others as we see needs. God is generous, so He wants us to be generous as well—and not only in buying gifts for our family at Christmastime. He wants us to give, even sacrificially, to people in real need.

> *Whoever shuts their ears to the cry of the poor will also cry out and not be answered.* PROVERBS 21:13 NIV

Does that sound like a threat? Really, it's an example of the biblical concept of sowing and reaping (Galatians 6:7–8). When you plant seeds of selfishness, you get back a crop of the same. But sow seeds of generosity? That's a whole different story.

Through the prophet Malachi, God shared this idea with His people, the Israelites. His words were specific to them but illustrate a truth that applies to all of us:

> *"Will a mere mortal rob God? Yet you rob me. But you ask, 'How are we robbing you?' In tithes and offerings. You are under a curse—your whole nation—because you are robbing me. Bring the whole tithe into the storehouse, that there may be food in my house. Test me in this," says the LORD Almighty, "and see if I will not throw open the floodgates of heaven and pour out so much blessing that there will not be room enough to store it."* MALACHI 3:8–10 NIV

TITHE = 10 PERCENT OF YOUR INCOME

The stingy guy hurts himself. The generous guy finds that God more than makes up what he gives away. You don't give to get—but when you give, freely and generously, God is happy to bless you in return.

A generous person will prosper; whoever refreshes others will be refreshed.
PROVERBS 11:25 NIV

Help me to trust in Your generosity, Lord. I want to give out of what You've already given me, helping meet the needs that You show me.

66 Our world isn't terribly fond of the Bible, but there's one verse most everyone can agree on: "Do not judge, or you too will be judged" (Matthew 7:1 NIV). These words of Jesus are like a sci-fi force field that repels every criticism of someone's behavior.

The reality, though, is a little more complicated than that—because the same Jesus who spoke the words above also said, "Stop judging by mere appearances, but instead judge correctly" (John 7:24 NIV).

For a no-regrets life, let's try to understand what Jesus meant.

DO THIS

Judge Correctly

It's so important to read Bible verses in context (see page 43). In the case of Matthew 7:1, the context occurs in the verses following:

> *"For in the same way you judge others, you will be judged, and with the measure you use, it will be measured to you. Why do you look at the speck of sawdust in your brother's eye and pay no attention to the plank in your own eye? How can you say to your brother, 'Let me take the speck out of your eye,' when all the time there is a plank in your own eye? You hypocrite, first take the plank out of your own eye, and then you will see clearly to remove the speck from your brother's eye."* MATTHEW 7:2–5 NIV

This world takes Matthew 7:1 to mean that you can't question anything people do—in fact, you'd better approve and celebrate it. But Jesus didn't say that at all. For one thing, He was speaking to people who follow Him ("brothers"). And Jesus indicated there *are* times when one Christian should challenge another to better living. That kind of judgment is helpful—unless the first guy is living sinfully himself. In that case, he needs to get that big blockage out of his own eye before trying to deal with a bit of dust in someone else's.

The apostle Paul also tackled hypocritical judging:

> *You, therefore, have no excuse, you who pass judgment on someone else, for at whatever point you judge another, you are condemning yourself, because you who pass judgment do the same things.* ROMANS 2:1 NIV

GOD *HATES* HYPOCRISY.

As Christians, we are absolutely not to criticize others for sins we ourselves are committing. Nor are we to assume what someone's inner motives are—that's something only God can do. But we can and should compare the behavior of others, Christian and non-Christian alike, to the standards of God's Word. For our fellow believers, we'll humbly encourage them to be more like Jesus. For the unsaved, we'll humbly point them to repentance and eternal life.

That's judging correctly.

> *Let us therefore make every effort to do what leads to peace and to mutual edification.*
> ROMANS 14:19 NIV

This is a tricky subject, Lord—please remind me to judge my own thoughts and actions first and then judge others only with an eye toward truly helping them.

67 An old saying claims that familiarity breeds contempt. What does that mean? That the people and places and things we know best can become dull and uninteresting to us. Human beings—always a rather discontented bunch—often want things to be "new and exciting." (Why do you think advertising harps on "new and exciting" so much?)

Beware of this tendency and fight it—especially if you get tired of important things like your family and church. . .or even God and your Christianity. Satan will aim every missile in his arsenal at you, and this *I'm bored* attitude is one of his most lethal. Since your faith is based on your knowledge of God through His Word,

DON'T DO THIS
Think the Bible Is Boring

Yes, the Bible is a big book—not many of us sit down to read twelve hundred pages at once. But Bible reading is not a sprint—it's a marathon. You have your entire lifetime, however much God gives you, to dig into this amazing book.

> *For the word of God is alive and active. Sharper than any double-edged sword, it penetrates even to dividing soul and spirit, joints and marrow; it judges the thoughts and attitudes of the heart.* HEBREWS 4:12 NIV

The Bible far surpasses any other book. While some writers entertain you or make you think, God's Word literally changes your life. For some people, it's instantaneous; for others (probably most), it's a longer process.

If you grew up in a Christian home and a good church, you probably heard the exciting stories of the Bible—of Moses and the plagues on Egypt, of God knocking down the walls of Jericho, of David whacking Goliath, of Jesus walking on water. If you met Jesus later, you may have been struck by God's compassion for broken human beings. Those things are highlights of scripture, but every word of the Bible has value.

> *Everything that was written in the past was written to teach us, so that through the endurance taught in the Scriptures and the encouragement they provide we might have hope.*
> ROMANS 15:4 NIV

COULDN'T WE ALL USE A LITTLE MORE HOPE?

Is it easy to read scripture? Some days, yes. . .other days, not at all. But it's incredibly important to your mental and spiritual health—so it's worth every effort you put into it.

As you spend time in scripture, you'll learn more about God—and what could be more interesting than knowing the Creator and keeper of all things, the infinite mind and power who defines reality?

Lazy minds say, "The Bible is boring." Don't go there—it only leads to regret. Commit to seeking God in scripture, and you will find Him.

Oh, how I love your law! I meditate on it all day long.
PSALM 119:97 NIV

Give me a hunger for Your Word, Lord.
I want to know You better!

68 You're a physical guy in a physical world. You eat real food, walk on a real earth, and soak up the rays of a real sun. You're as natural—in the sense of being a part of nature—as everything else.

But there's more to life than just nature. You have the opportunity to rise above what is normal, typical, and expected. In fact, you can

DO THIS

Be Supernatural

In today's culture, *supernatural* often means creepy, freaky, demonic. But for Christians, it just means you draw on the wisdom and strength of God, who transcends nature in every way—because He created it. How else could you live as Jesus described in His Sermon on the Mount?

> *"You have heard that it has been said, 'You shall love your neighbor and hate your enemy.' But I say to you, love your enemies, bless those who curse you, do good to those who hate you, and pray for those who despitefully use you and persecute you, that you may be the children of your Father who is in heaven. For He makes His sun to rise on the evil and on the good, and sends rain on the just and on the unjust. For if you love those who love you, what reward do you have? Don't even the tax collectors do the same? And if you greet your brothers only, what do you do more than others? Don't even the tax collectors do so? Therefore you be perfect, even as your Father who is in heaven is perfect."* MATTHEW 5:43–48 SKJV

Love my enemies? Pray for people who hate me? Be perfect like God Himself?

Yeah, that's not natural at all. But if God commands something, it *can* be done. How? Not by the force of your own will, not by any amount of effort or self-sacrifice. . .but only by God's Holy Spirit inside you.

> I bow my knees to the Father of our Lord Jesus Christ, from whom the whole family in heaven and earth is named, that He would grant you, according to the riches of His glory, to be strengthened with might by His Spirit in the inner man.
> EPHESIANS 3:14–16 SKJV

GOD HAS INFINITE POWER TO SPREAD AROUND.

You will regret trying to live the Christian life in your own power—that leads only to hypocrisy, frustration, and burnout. God Himself will provide the strength you need to accomplish all He wants for you. It takes time to fully understand that, so keep praying, studying your Bible, and interacting with older, wiser believers. In time, God's Spirit will make you supernatural.

> **"Not by might, nor by power, but by My Spirit," says the LORD of hosts.**
> ZECHARIAH 4:6 SKJV

I need Your Spirit, Lord, to help me rise above my natural self. Please fill me with Your love, power, and purity so I can be truly supernatural.

69 The year 1976 was quite remarkable. It included the United States' two hundredth anniversary, the start of filming for the movie *Star Wars,* the founding of the Apple Computer Company, and the birth of Twitter founder Jack Dorsey. Oh, and there was also the introduction of a marvelously descriptive name for lazy, apathetic TV watchers.

Decades later, that two-word phrase still works. It's spoken in fun (usually), but you really don't want it applied to you. With life so full of really important stuff, here's a good rule for avoiding regrets:

DON'T DO THIS

Be a Couch Potato

The phrase was coined by a group of friends who preferred to sit on the sofa, eat junk food, and watch television rather than join in the health and exercise boom of the 1970s. Back then, TVs produced images by way of cathode-ray tubes—and the people watching soon realized that their self-assigned "tuber" nickname was another term for "potato." The rest, as they say, is history.

Today's devices are way beyond those old CRT screens. But the temptation to lie around, eat junk, and watch stuff for hours on end is just the same as ever. Hmm, wonder what God's Word might have to say about that?

> *"Physical training is good, but training for godliness is much better, promising benefits in this life and in the life to come."*
> 1 TIMOTHY 4:8 NLT

The Bible doesn't say a lot about exercise, maybe because physical exertion was the norm in Bible times—people got a good workout just walking from place to place, planting and harvesting their crops, and building houses and furniture and other things entirely by hand. The apostle Paul, who often used athletic events as examples for Christian living, gave a thumbs-up to physical exercise in the verse above. But he also called for mental and spiritual exercise, as he did again in the verse below:

> *Study to show yourself approved to God, a workman who does not need to be ashamed, rightly dividing the word of truth.* 2 TIMOTHY 2:15 SKJV

EVER NOTICE HOW OFTEN THE BIBLE COMMANDS *WORK*?
NOT TO BE SAVED, BUT TO GROW IN GRACE AFTER YOU'RE SAVED.

Everything you are—body, mind, and spirit—is the gift of God. You'll be happiest and most influential when you take care of each aspect of your personality. Don't be a couch potato in any sense of the term. Far more important things await you.

What, do you not know that your body is the temple of the Holy Spirit, who is in you, whom you have from God, and you are not your own? For you were bought with a price. Therefore glorify God in your body and in your spirit, which are God's.
1 CORINTHIANS 6:19–20 SKJV

It's so easy to be lazy, Lord—but I want to keep my body, mind, and spirit in shape for You. Please help me to get up and push myself to bigger and better things.

70 People are awful. They gossip and insult and bully others. . .and those are some of the nicer things they do. All through society, we see far too many hateful, harmful people, those who lie, cheat, steal, and kill. Old and young, rich and poor, male and female—anyone, it seems, can be an absolute disgrace to humanity.

And yet. . . Every person, no matter how selfish, mean, or destructive, was made by God. And every one of them is *potentially* a child of God through faith in Jesus Christ.

We will often be saddened, frustrated, and angered by the bad behavior of other people. But we'll be better people ourselves (and more like Jesus) if we

DO THIS

Look for God's Image in All

You probably know that when God made human beings, He did it "in our image, in our likeness" (Genesis 1:26 NIV—that plural pronoun *our* hints at the Trinity). The same verse indicates that the image of God in people allowed them to "rule over" other living things. Being made in God's image sets us apart from the animals.

After the flood, God gave Noah some new rules, including the freedom to kill and eat animals—but if anyone killed a human being, there would be a heavy penalty:

> *"Whoever sheds human blood, by humans shall their blood be shed; for in the image of God has God made mankind."*
> GENESIS 9:6 NIV

Of course, God's image in people can be hard to see. Even the best of us are sinful and selfish—we don't always do right. But we should still look for the image of our Lord in every person we meet. Think of the Old Testament hero David—he'd already been anointed to be king of Israel, but the current king, Saul, was pursuing David to kill him. Given a chance to turn the tables, David said no—because God's view of Saul carried much more weight than his own.

> "This day you [Saul] have seen with your own eyes how the Lord delivered you into my hands in the cave. Some urged me to kill you, but I spared you; I said, 'I will not lay my hand on my lord, because he is the Lord's anointed.' " 1 Samuel 24:10 niv

READ THIS WHOLE CHAPTER—IT'S AN INTERESTING STORY.

The point is this: only God knows who will ultimately believe in Jesus and be saved. We shouldn't try to make that decision for Him, even with people who seem the furthest gone. Let's never regret writing off somebody who could one day be a brother.

The Lord is not slow in keeping his promise, as some understand slowness. Instead he is patient with you, not wanting anyone to perish, but everyone to come to repentance.

2 Peter 3:9 niv

This is a tough one, Lord—but I ask You to help me see Your image in everyone I meet.

71 How would you define the word *atheist*? An atheist is simply a person who doesn't believe in God. The Bible calls that kind of person a fool (Psalm 14:1).

There is no such thing as a "Christian atheist." True followers of Jesus recognize Him as the Son of God—but just as importantly, *as God*, because He is one with God (John 10:30).

And yet even Christian guys can sometimes fall into what some call a "practical atheism"—that is, a kind of atheism in everyday life. It's not that they don't believe in God; they just don't acknowledge Him for all He truly is. To avoid regrets in this area,

DON'T DO THIS
Limit God

We limit God when we doubt His omniscience (His total knowledge), His omnipotence (His complete power), and His omnipresence (His absolute everywhereness). Limiting God in these ways is dangerous, since we might be tempted to sin against Him. If we don't think He's always with us or aware of what we're doing, we could find ourselves on a bad path, doing our own thing.

You've heard the story of Job, haven't you? God allowed Satan to attack Job, a very good man with a lot of wealth and a large family, all of which he lost. . .along with his own health. Though he never turned against God, Job certainly questioned the Lord's knowledge and power. In the end, after God had proved how infinitely superior He was to Job, the man admitted,

> *"I know that you can do all things; no purpose of yours can be thwarted."* JOB 42:2 NIV

NEVER FORGET THAT THIS AMAZING GOD IS ON THE SIDE OF EVERYONE WHO FOLLOWS JESUS.

The ancient Israelites often limited God in their minds. They chose to follow worthless idols instead of the one true God who had created the raw materials that made up the idols. God was insulted and angry:

> *"Do people make their own gods? Yes, but they are not gods! Therefore I will teach them—this time I will teach them my power and might. Then they will know that my name is the* LORD." JEREMIAH 16:20–21 NIV

Let's remind ourselves—regularly—of God's incredible "beyondness." He is everywhere, with all knowledge and infinite power. And even when He doesn't seem to be engaged or moving in our lives, the reality is this: our God is limitless. Never, consciously or unconsciously, limit Him in your mind.

Now to the King eternal, immortal, invisible, the only God, be honor and glory for ever and ever. Amen.
1 TIMOTHY 1:17 NIV

Lord God, I know You made the universe and You keep it by Your will. I know You made me and You offered me salvation when I was a rebellious sinner. I praise You for Your limitless goodness. Help me to honor You in every part of my life.

72 Imagine this: You've gone out of your way to help someone. You have spent a considerable amount of your time and energy, and even some of your money, to see the project through. When it's all done, the other person turns on his heel and walks away without a word of thanks.

None of us should do good deeds in order to receive gratitude—but it sure seems wrong when a simple thank-you is nowhere to be found.

To be fair, there have probably been times when each of us has received other people's kindness without a proper acknowledgment. Let's make sure, from today forward, that we never go down that path. Let's be sure to

DO THIS
Be Thankful

In the New International Version of the Bible, forms of the words *thanks* and *grateful* appear nearly 140 times. Seems like kind of an important idea.

More than kind of important, actually. The apostle Paul says gratitude is one of God's greatest desires for His children:

> *Give thanks in all circumstances; for this is God's will for you in Christ Jesus.* 1 THESSALONIANS 5:18 NIV

God's will is for followers of Jesus to be thankful. Not necessarily *for* every circumstance, but *in* every circumstance. When a loved one dies, you won't be thankful for the loss—but you can be grateful for the relationship you enjoyed. And with fellow believers, you can be very thankful for the promise of heaven.

Today's world is characterized by attitudes like greed,

competition, and victimhood more than it is characterized by gratitude. But God knows best (He *always* does) that a thankful spirit makes people healthier and happier.

> Let the peace of Christ rule in your hearts, since as members of one body you were called to peace. And be thankful.
> COLOSSIANS 3:15 NIV

GRATITUDE AND PEACE FIT TOGETHER BEAUTIFULLY.

Today, right now, fire up your "thanks radar." Consciously look for reasons to express gratitude, to your parents, siblings, friends, fellow students, coworkers, even total strangers who open a door or pick up something you dropped.

And over and above all of those people, be sure you say thanks to God. He gave you life. He gave you family and friends. He ultimately provides your food and clothing and health and strength. He chose you, even before He created the universe, to know His Son, Jesus Christ, and be saved.

Every human being, and especially every Christian, has much to thank God for. Don't regret sliding into a negative, depressed mindset. Try this instead:

> **Enter his gates with thanksgiving and his courts with praise; give thanks to him and praise his name.**
> **PSALM 100:4 NIV**

Thank You, Lord, for everything—especially for Your patience with me when I haven't always been grateful. Please tune my spirit to kindnesses—from You and other people—so I can be quick to say thanks.

73 Ever been around a big talker? No matter what's being discussed, this guy is an expert. He knows all about everything—or at least that's what he wants you to think. But it doesn't take long to figure him out. Though he's offering hot-shot commentary on every imaginable topic, it soon becomes clear that he's just full of hot air.

That's the extreme case. But at one time or another, *all* of us are tempted to act like we're smarter or more experienced than we really are. Others will see through our act too, no matter how hard we try. So to avoid regrets,

DON'T DO THIS
Pretend to Be Someone You're Not

Often the temptation to act like an expert is driven by fear. Guys don't want others to think less of them, so they act like they know all about car engines. . .or hard rock bands. . .or this week's NFL leaders. . .or girls. Somehow, we have to fit in with the crowd, so we try to talk the other guys' language and maintain their attention. But in the end, it's always better to just be yourself.

Of course, this fear goes both ways. We might pretend we're part of a particular crowd, or we may want to pretend we're *not*. That was Simon Peter's problem on the night his friend Jesus was arrested:

> Peter was sitting out in the courtyard, and a servant girl came to him. "You also were with Jesus of Galilee," she said. But he denied it before them all. "I don't know what you're talking about," he said. MATTHEW 26:69–70 NIV

That's pretty bad. But the story gets even worse.

> *Then he went out to the gateway, where another servant girl saw him and said to the people there, "This fellow was with Jesus of Nazareth." He denied it again, with an oath: "I don't know the man!" After a little while, those standing there went up to Peter and said, "Surely you are one of them; your accent gives you away." Then he began to call down curses, and he swore to them, "I don't know the man!"*
> MATTHEW 26:71–74 NIV

THIS AFTER INSISTING, "EVEN IF ALL FALL AWAY ON ACCOUNT OF YOU, I NEVER WILL" (MATTHEW 26:33 NIV)

In the moment of crisis, Peter pretended he *wasn't* a friend and follower of Jesus. In reality, he was both—and acting as if he wasn't led to crushing regret. Immediately after Peter's final denial, a rooster crowed. "Then Peter remembered the word Jesus had spoken: 'Before the rooster crows, you will disown me three times' " (Matthew 26:75 NIV). He rushed away and cried.

Be true to yourself, in every situation. Sure, it might be uncomfortable at times. . .but isn't that better than the alternative?

> *Fear of man will prove to be a snare, but whoever trusts in the LORD is kept safe.*
> PROVERBS 29:25 NIV

I want to be real, Lord, every time, everywhere. May I never pretend to be anything other than what I am.

74 So what do you think about school?

Some guys love it, some guys hate it. Most guys are probably somewhere in between. Maybe math is kind of fun but history makes you snooze. Maybe the extracurricular activities are more important to you than classes. Maybe you'd much rather do hands-on courses at a vocational center.

It's okay if school really isn't your thing—a lot of people struggle through their formal education and still become very successful adults. Of course, it's okay too if you *love* school and can't wait to get to your next class. Whatever the case may be, recognize this truth: school is temporary, but learning is forever.

Well, learning *should* be forever. Here's an important rule for you:

DO THIS

Be a Lifelong Learner

Have you ever said to yourself, "Why am I learning [insert course name here]? I'll never use this again!" Maybe. But (a) you could be surprised to find that knowledge coming in handy someday, and (b) just the practice of learning will serve you well through life.

We're not just talking about algebra and chemistry and literature and art appreciation. Your Christian life is all about ongoing learning—which brings its own rewards. Here's a classic quotation from Jesus Himself:

> *"Come to me, all you who are weary and burdened, and I will give you rest. Take my yoke upon you and learn from me, for I am gentle and humble in heart, and you will find rest for your souls."* MATTHEW 11:28–29 NIV

LEARN FROM JESUS TO FIND REST!

Think about this: mental laziness can bring on stress. How? Well, if you don't stay on top of your schoolwork, you'll feel more pressure at test time. If you don't keep up with developments in your job field, you'll fall behind your coworkers. If you don't study the Bible and grow in your knowledge of God, you won't enjoy all the benefits He offers you—because they come by faith. How can you claim biblical promises you don't know?

Never think learning is only for the "smart" people. Even worse, don't think it's just for nerds or weaklings. Even Jesus was a learner!

> *"I have called you friends, for everything that I learned from my Father I have made known to you."* JOHN 15:15 NIV

You may not sense it now—teen guys often don't—but ongoing learning is hugely important to a good life. It will give you a better job and keep you advancing in your career. It will help you better understand and relate to people. And it will keep you moving toward God, in whose presence you'll learn for all eternity.

> *And Jesus grew in wisdom and stature,*
> *and in favor with God and man.*
> LUKE 2:52 NIV

Lord, give me a hunger for learning—not so I can impress people with my brains, but so I can live a truly good life.

75 Don't you love it when the bad guy in a movie gets what's coming to him? Mr. Trouble has been causing grief for ninety minutes, but now the hero has completely turned the tables. If you were the star of the show, would you stick your finger in the bad guy's face and laugh?

Now, how about in real life? What if you turned the tables on an obnoxious opponent in sports or some other extracurricular activity? Or on the guy who stole your girlfriend? Would you take the opportunity to rub your victory in his face?

Bad idea.

God has a pretty strong opinion on this issue, and it isn't "pay the other guy back with epic mockery." Whatever you do,

DON'T DO THIS
Gloat

People talk about "karma," which actually has some parallels to the biblical idea of sowing and reaping. Bad guys sow bad seeds and reap really bad crops. Great, right? Let's enjoy the show!

But when *you* sow the bad seeds of angry, vengeful reactions, you'll reap a bad crop yourself. Here's how Solomon—inspired by God's Spirit—described the process:

> *Do not gloat when your enemy falls; when they stumble, do not let your heart rejoice, or the LORD will see and disapprove and turn his wrath away from them.* PROVERBS 24:17–18 NIV

God *always* sees, so don't think you can sneak any gloating past Him.

The Lord applied this rule in a big way to the nation of Edom. That was a people group descended from Esau, the older twin brother of Jacob, the forefather of Israel. If you recall, the two boys had a rocky relationship—and the nations they began did too. When Babylonian soldiers under King Nebuchadnezzar ransacked Jerusalem in 586 BC, the Edomites gloated. And God was not pleased.

> "Because of the violence against your brother Jacob, you will be covered with shame; you will be destroyed forever. On the day you stood aloof while strangers carried off his wealth and foreigners entered his gates and cast lots for Jerusalem, you were like one of them. You should not gloat over your brother in the day of his misfortune." OBADIAH 10–12 NIV

THERE'S STILL AN ISRAEL TODAY, BUT NO EDOM....

We can (and should) pray for God's justice, which He will ultimately dispense with perfect fairness. But we should never enjoy anybody's downfall. Don't bring trouble on yourself by gloating. Always show people the same grace that God has shown you.

Pride goes before destruction, a haughty spirit before a fall.
PROVERBS 16:18 NIV

*It's so human to enjoy seeing troublemakers fall,
Lord—but I need to be superhuman, showing Your
love and grace to all. Please fill my heart with
compassion, even for the worst of people.*

76 Earlier generations of believers debated whether the United States was a "Christian nation." While there was never a time when every American truly followed Jesus, some people argued that the laws, institutions, political leadership—and population— possessed a general respect for the Christian faith. As a whole, most Americans "spoke the same language" on moral issues, a language that sounded a lot like the Bible's.

Of course, there have always been people who fight against that. In the 1960s, for example, many young people resisted those cultural norms, and "sex, drugs, and rock and roll" became a way to stick it to the man—"the man" being that supposedly Christian culture.

Well, if American culture ever was Christian, it becomes less and less so by the minute. Now, followers of Jesus are like the hippies and protesters of old, standing out from society like the proverbial sore thumb. When most people are rebelling against God, don't just go with the flow—

DO THIS

Be Countercultural

As a prefix, *counter* indicates contrary or opposite. Being countercultural just means you're not like most of the people around you.

That's what God has always wanted for His people. But the Old Testament Israelites, sadly, preferred to follow the ways of the sinful nations nearby. Though God was truly their King, the people marched up to His spokesman Samuel and said,

> *"We want a king over us. Then we will be like all the other nations."* 1 SAMUEL 8:19–20 NIV

God gave them what they wanted. But read through 1 and 2 Kings to see how it worked out: even the best kings were flawed, the worst ones atrocious. Israel lived to regret being like "all the other nations."

You live in the Christian era, after the life, death, and resurrection of Jesus. His kingdom is spiritual, one you enter by simple faith. Like ancient Israel, you *should* keep a certain distance from those who are not God's people:

> *Do not be yoked together with unbelievers. For what do righteousness and wickedness have in common? Or what fellowship can light have with darkness?* 2 CORINTHIANS 6:14 NIV

PAUL WENT ON TO ASK, "WHAT DOES A BELIEVER HAVE IN COMMON WITH AN UNBELIEVER?" (VERSE 15 NIV).

Of course you'll have unsaved acquaintances, classmates, neighbors, coworkers. But your deepest relationships—your best friend, your girlfriend (who could one day be your wife), your business partners—really should be committed Christians. You'll need support to avoid the regret that comes with being like the world. You'll want to be truly countercultural.

As God has said: "I will live with them and walk among them, and I will be their God, and they will be my people." Therefore, "Come out from them and be separate, says the Lord."
2 CORINTHIANS 6:16–17 NIV

Heavenly Father, I know I am in this world, but I can't be of it. Please help me to be countercultural—not to show that I'm better than anyone else but to honor You.

77 There's a real tug-of-war going on in churches these days. There's a growing divide between those who take the Bible at face value and others who think God's Word needs to be "updated" for modern people.

In many cases, the issue is sexual morality. For the first nineteen centuries after Jesus lived on earth, nearly every Christian church agreed that sex should be reserved for marriage, and marriage was a covenant (a formal, binding agreement) between one man, one woman, and God. But in recent decades, society has pretty much nuked that idea. Even many churches, out of a desire not to offend people, have gone along—a little or a lot.

Issues like this are anything but trivial. Mess up here, and you'll definitely regret it. To stay on the right and good path,

DON'T DO THIS
"Modernize" Your Faith

The little New Testament letter of Jude is all about false teaching, which is a change, an update, a modernizing of "the faith that God has entrusted once for all time to his holy people" (Jude 3 NLT). Jude urged his readers to "defend" that faith.

The apostle Paul sent a similar message to the Christians of Galatia. He could hardly believe that they were straying away from the plain message they'd received:

> *I am shocked that you are turning away so soon from God, who called you to himself through the loving mercy of Christ. You are following a different way that pretends to be the Good News but is not the Good News at all. You are being fooled by those who deliberately twist the truth concerning Christ.* GALATIANS 1:6–7 NLT

Not everyone who claims to be Christian is. (Here's an interesting little study: look up how many times the New Testament mentions "false prophets" and "false teachers.") That's why it's so important to test every message you hear against the Bible, *which does not change*. God has given us the rule book, and its word is final.

> *Let God's curse fall on anyone, including us or even an angel from heaven, who preaches a different kind of Good News than the one we preached to you. I say again what we have said before: If anyone preaches any other Good News than the one you welcomed, let that person be cursed.* GALATIANS 1:8–9 NLT

STRONG WORDS FROM PAUL

Beware of "fresh new ideas" about God's Word. Beware of changing your understanding of scripture to align with some cultural viewpoint. That's not good for you or anyone else who needs to know God's unchanging truth.

Obviously, I'm not trying to win the approval of people, but of God. If pleasing people were my goal, I would not be Christ's servant.

GALATIANS 1:10 NLT

Lord, there's so much pressure to conform to this world—but I want to be transformed by You. Keep me faithful to Your unchanging Word.

78 Isn't it cool to be "pleasantly surprised"? Once in a while, people do more than expected to make a situation better:

Jack needed a new muffler on his car. The local mechanic made the repair. . .and also gave the car a wash.

Andrew was distributing flyers about his missing dog. A retired neighbor promised to keep an eye out. . .and offered to knock on doors the next street over.

Xavier hoped to attend a prestigious summer music program. His band director provided a written reference. . .and also paid the application fee.

In a self-centered world, even the smallest kindnesses shine brightly. Here's a great way to enhance any human interaction:

DO THIS

Go Above and Beyond

We should serve other people gladly and well, because doing so reflects our kind and generous God. In the area of service—as with giving—we'll find that obedience often brings blessing back to us. We don't give or serve simply to get something in return. . .but done with the right attitude, above-and-beyond service does have a reward:

> Do you see someone skilled in their work? They will serve before kings; they will not serve before officials of low rank.
> PROVERBS 22:29 NIV

DOING MORE THAN EXPECTED WILL ALSO BE GOOD FOR YOUR CAREER.

No king is higher than God, who gives us skills and abilities to benefit His people, the church, the "body of Christ." And He calls us to be generous with our time, our talents, and our resources.

Being selfish—or simply oblivious—makes your world smaller and leads to regret. So whether you're dealing with your family, a boss and coworkers, fellow students, church people, or complete strangers, always do more than expected. Actively seek out ways to go above and beyond. Your selflessness, generosity, and good work will upgrade every situation and reflect well on the God you serve.

What good is it, my brothers and sisters, if someone claims to have faith but has no deeds? Can such faith save them? Suppose a brother or a sister is without clothes and daily food. If one of you says to them, "Go in peace; keep warm and well fed," but does nothing about their physical needs, what good is it? In the same way, faith by itself, if it is not accompanied by action, is dead. But someone will say, "You have faith; I have deeds." Show me your faith without deeds, and I will show you my faith by my deeds.
JAMES 2:14–18 NIV

Open my eyes, Lord, to opportunities to do more than other people expect. Then give me the will to follow through. I want to reflect Your kindness and generosity in everything I do.

79 "If all your friends jumped off a cliff, would you jump too?" Has a parent or teacher or youth leader ever thrown this zinger at you? If they haven't, they should.

Generations of kids have heard this from older, wiser adults. It's a memorable warning against peer pressure—don't do everything your buddies are doing, because they might be doing something dumb. And not only your buddies, but culture as a whole.

A pile of broken people, regretting their choices, lies at the bottom of that cliff. Be smarter than they were.

DON'T DO THIS
Conform to the World

Conform: to be equal or identical to, to be in agreement or harmony with. (Thank you, Merriam-Webster.) Christians know—through God's Word and by hard experience—that this world is a messed-up, sinful place. And that realization grows the older you get. Teen guys, with a little less perspective and a larger sense of invincibility, can go down a bad path fast. So it's wise to listen to older Christians' warnings—as well as their advice.

> *Do not conform to the pattern of this world, but be transformed by the renewing of your mind. Then you will be able to test and approve what God's will is—his good, pleasing and perfect will.* ROMANS 12:2 NIV

That is the apostle Paul's classic teaching on conforming (to the world) versus transforming (your life by the knowledge of God). It follows the equally classic verse 1 (NIV): "I urge you, brothers and sisters, in view of God's mercy, to offer your bodies as a living sacrifice, holy and pleasing to God—this is your true and proper worship." Notice the active, personal terms: *you* should "offer" yourself, *you* should "not conform," *you* should "be transformed" by the renewing of *your* mind. God is the ultimate power in this, but you need to play a willing role.

Here is some more advice for you, also from Paul:

> *Flee the evil desires of youth and pursue righteousness, faith, love and peace, along with those who call on the Lord out of a pure heart.* 2 TIMOTHY 2:22 NIV

MORE ACTIVE, PERSONAL VERBS: *FLEE, PURSUE*

We began by asking, "If all your friends jumped off a cliff, would you jump too?" Notice in 2 Timothy that one key to avoiding a foolish, dangerous conformity to the world is to have good, Christian friends—"those who call on the Lord out of a pure heart."

Choose your friends carefully, and never let the world squeeze you into its own mold, as Bible translator J. B. Phillips famously put Romans 12:2. Be transformed, not conformed.

Don't you know that friendship with the world means enmity against God? Therefore, anyone who chooses to be a friend of the world becomes an enemy of God.

JAMES 4:4 NIV

I want to stand out from this world, Lord, by my kind, respectful, honest, and pure behavior.

80 Can you name the fifty states and their capitals? Could you recite Abraham Lincoln's Gettysburg Address? Have you committed any poetry of William Shakespeare or Alfred, Lord Tennyson to memory? At times in US history, these were relatively common expectations for students.

Whew, some guys may think. *Good thing they haven't asked me to do that—I'm just not very good at memorizing.*

But many of those same guys probably have tons of sports statistics, song lyrics, movie lines, and other "important details" stored away in their minds. Often, what we keep in our brains comes down to what we care about most.

As Christians, we should really care about the Bible, since it tells us all we need to know about God and our relationship to Him. Here's a pursuit you'll never regret:

DO THIS

Memorize Scripture

Oh, sure, there are zillions of Bibles out there—you probably have several in your house right now. And these days you can read every imaginable translation online, anywhere you have cell service or Wi-Fi. You can look up any scripture at any time. . .but there's something special about *memorizing* important verses. Here's perhaps the most special thing of all:

Your word have I hidden in my heart, that I might not sin against You. PSALM 119:11 SKJV

NEW TO MEMORIZING SCRIPTURE? START WITH THIS VERSE!

God's Word is unlike any other book. As Hebrews 4:12 (SKJV) tells us, it's "living and powerful." The Bible isn't just inspiring; it's inspired (meaning "breathed out") by God Himself. When read and studied and put into practice, it truly changes lives.

And when scripture is memorized, it's always available to meet the need of the moment—even if you left your hard copy at home and your phone battery is dead. Your access to God's Word goes way beyond what the ancient Israelites enjoyed. . .but God's instruction to them also applies to you:

> *"You shall lay up these words of Mine in your heart and in your soul. . . . And you shall teach them to your children, speaking of them when you sit in your house and when you walk by the way, when you lie down and when you rise up."*
> DEUTERONOMY 11:18–19 SKJV

Even when Bibles are plentiful, memorizing God's Word will add power and beauty to your life. And if for some reason Bibles aren't readily available? Well, then you'll really be happy to have hidden God's Word in your heart.

Let the word of Christ dwell in you richly in all wisdom, teaching and admonishing one another in psalms and hymns and spiritual songs, singing with grace in your hearts to the Lord.
COLOSSIANS 3:16 SKJV

Lord, I can remember all kinds of less important things—now please help me to commit Your Word to my memory.

81 In his early seventies, a successful Christian businessman recalled his dad fondly. The elder man had been a humble farmer—but his Christian faith and practical wisdom laid a strong foundation for the life his son would build.

One of the father's sayings stayed with the son for decades: "If you don't start, you don't have to stop." What did he mean by that? If you say no whenever you're tempted to do wrong, you'll never find yourself regretting a bad habit or an out-and-out addiction. Here's a powerful rule to follow:

DON'T DO THIS
Start Something You Can't Stop

Some of the things to avoid are obvious: don't start drinking, don't take the drug you're offered, don't look at porn. But choices of seemingly less consequence can also form bad habits—so don't lie to get out of trouble, don't disrespect authority, don't choose video games or overeating or laziness when there's a better way to go. Really, the list is as varied as the people in this world.

Maybe you've memorized the nine "fruits of the Spirit" mentioned in the book of Galatians. The last one—self-control—gets an interesting twist in the New Life Version of the Bible:

> *The fruit that comes from having the Holy Spirit in our lives is: love, joy, peace, not giving up, being kind, being good, having faith, being gentle, and being the boss over our own desires.* GALATIANS 5:22–23 NLV

CHECK OUT GALATIANS 5:19-21 TO SEE WHAT LIFE LOOKS LIKE APART FROM GOD'S SPIRIT.

Your desires will tell you all kinds of things that contradict the Bible. And the world around you will support those desires. But God is pleased when "you're the boss"—when you consciously reject your feelings in favor of His clearly stated will. Since you're still young, this is the perfect time to build your self-control muscles—to not *start* things you'll need to *stop* later.

> So do not let sin have power over your body here on earth. You must not obey the body and let it do what it wants to do. Do not give any part of your body for sinful use. Instead, give yourself to God as a living person who has been raised from the dead. Give every part of your body to God to do what is right. ROMANS 6:12–13 NLV

Don't be shocked if you occasionally fail—we all do. But when you give in to temptation, make sure you confess to God right away. Then commit yourself again to letting His Spirit lead your life. Don't start habits that will be tough to stop as you get older.

> *I say this to you: Let the Holy Spirit lead you in each step. Then you will not please your sinful old selves.*
> GALATIANS 5:16 NLV

I need wisdom and strength to avoid temptation, Lord—but I know You have wisdom and strength in abundance. Please guide me in Your ways.

82 What kind of guy gets the most attention in our world? Top athletes, for sure. Very wealthy men. Good-looking actors and models. Sometimes guys who are just famous for being famous. (Social media can be so weird.)

How about a wise guy? No, not the smart aleck, but the guy who truly understands things. He's not typically as visible or celebrated, but the world needs him—and a lot more like him.

While it's popular to be handsome, rich, talented, and famous, those traits aren't as lasting and beneficial as being wise. On your path to a no-regrets life, make a commitment to

DO THIS

Pursue Wisdom

Wisdom isn't necessarily intelligence. A guy can be born with a world-class brain and still be a real dummy. That's because wisdom goes beyond just information—it's knowledge about the world and the way things work and the application of that knowledge to make life better. And here's good news: wisdom is something anyone can pursue and develop:

> *Get wisdom. Get understanding. Do not forget it or turn away from the words of my mouth. Do not forsake her, and she shall preserve you. Love her, and she shall keep you. Wisdom is the principal thing. Therefore, get wisdom, and with all your getting, get understanding.* PROVERBS 4:5–7 SKJV

PRINCIPAL = MOST IMPORTANT OR CONSEQUENTIAL

Those are the words of Solomon, king of Israel, to his own sons. Years before, at his request, God had given Solomon wisdom—so much wisdom "that there has been none like you before you, nor shall any arise like you after you" (1 Kings 3:12 SKJV). At that time, Solomon was following his own teaching found later in the book of Proverbs:

> *The fear of the LORD is the beginning of wisdom, and the knowledge of the holy is understanding.* PROVERBS 9:10 SKJV

You may recall that Solomon lost his wisdom along the way by marrying a few women (well, seven hundred of them) and ultimately worshipping their false gods. What a tragic implosion for a man who started so well—it points to the absolute importance of keeping God front and center in your thoughts.

The "fear of the Lord" is a deep respect and awe for who He is, and it puts you on the path of wisdom. Then the "knowledge of the holy"—from the time you spend in Bible study and prayer—grows your understanding.

Few things in life are more important than wisdom. Make sure you don't neglect its pursuit. Get it! Got it?

If any of you lacks wisdom, let him ask of God, who gives to all men generously and without reproach, and it shall be given him.
JAMES 1:5 SKJV

Lord, I can always use more wisdom. Please grant me an ever-growing understanding of You and Your Word so that I can live well and help others do the same.

83 Maybe you've seen it in a cartoon or a movie: someone does something wrong and God zaps them to ashes.

The old lightning bolt trick is usually played for a laugh. But a touch of real fear may be driving it. Deep down, people know that God exists, that He's powerful, and that they're somehow separated from Him (see Romans 1:18–32). It's not a big jump to start thinking, *God is out to get me.*

Let's figure this one out, because there's a potentially eternal regret hanging in the balance. Whether you already follow Jesus or not,

DON'T DO THIS
Think God Hates You

That lightning-bolt-from-God idea probably arose from certain Bible stories—of God raining down fire on Sodom and Gomorrah, of God sending down fire on Elijah's sacrifice at Mount Carmel, of God striking badly behaving people with leprosy. There's no doubt that God is deadly serious about sin. . .but the overall message of the Bible is that He's also very happy to accept anyone who turns away from their sin. God actually pleaded with His people, the Israelites, to leave their idols and return to Him:

> *"As I live," says the Lord GOD, "I have no pleasure in the death of the wicked but that the wicked turns from his way and lives. Turn, turn from your evil ways, for why will you die, O house of Israel?"* EZEKIEL 33:11 SKJV

In Ezekiel's day, the life and work of Jesus Christ was still centuries in the future. The Israelites needed to obey God's commands, showing their faith by the things they did. Today, though, we look back on Jesus' death on the cross, seeing and believing in His perfect work on our behalf. Jesus' sacrifice for our sin was certainly not the strategy of an angry God who just wants to destroy people.

> *But God demonstrates His love toward us, in that while we were still sinners, Christ died for us.* ROMANS 5:8 SKJV

WE ARE SAVED FROM GOD'S "WRATH" AGAINST SIN WHEN WE FOLLOW JESUS (VERSE 9).

Now, if sin is serious enough to demand Jesus' death on the cross (and it is), we don't dare mess with it. If you haven't already believed in Jesus, do that. . .soon. If you are a follower of Jesus, then avoid even the "appearance of evil" (1 Thessalonians 5:22 SKJV). Sin is a destroyer, both now and forever—but God gives you a wide-open door of escape.

Don't ever think God hates you. He wants you as His much-loved son.

> *Behold, what manner of love the Father has bestowed on us, that we should be called the sons of God.*
> 1 JOHN 3:1 SKJV

Wow, Lord God, thank You for loving me even when I was a sinner. I believe in Jesus' sacrifice for sin—my sin—and commit myself to following Him in faith. Why should I ever think You hate me?

84 It's a common plot element in movies and TV shows: someone sees or hears something, misunderstands what's happening, and responds in a totally inappropriate way. That's a great basis for comedy, as writers and producers wring laughs out of the awkward tension that results.

Unfortunately, those misunderstandings aren't usually as funny in real life. In fact, they can really hurt people. Here's a great rule for avoiding the regret they bring:

DON'T DO THIS
Jump to Conclusions

How often do we assume the worst about people and the situations they find themselves in? It seems something in our human nature drives us to a negative reaction first—maybe that's because our sinful nature is a selfish nature, and we automatically believe we are better than others.

But we're certainly not the "bigger man" when we judge unfairly—like the Old Testament priest Eli did with a godly, childless woman who was begging the Lord for a son:

> *Hannah was praying in her heart, and her lips were moving but her voice was not heard. Eli thought she was drunk and said to her, "How long are you going to stay drunk? Put away your wine."* 1 SAMUEL 1:13–14 NIV

To his credit, Eli listened when Hannah explained herself, and he sent her away with a blessing. But Eli never should have jumped to such a negative conclusion in the first place.

Centuries later, a future apostle of Jesus went down in history for his careless, snap reaction to the Messiah and Savior of the world:

> *Philip found Nathanael and told him, "We have found the one Moses wrote about in the Law, and about whom the prophets also wrote—Jesus of Nazareth, the son of Joseph." "Nazareth! Can anything good come from there?" Nathanael asked.* JOHN 1:45–46 NIV

NATHANAEL CHANGED HIS TUNE PRETTY QUICKLY.

Philip simply replied, "Come and see" (verse 46 NIV), and to *his* credit, Nathanael checked out the guy from that hick town (verses 47–51). As it turns out, yes—something very good could come from Nazareth.

Today, be especially careful of your reaction to stuff you see online. Remember that you can't read the tone of a typed message, so your quick, negative reply might be totally off base. Beware of people who intentionally post false information—deceptive words, photoshopped pictures, or AI video—just to stir up trouble (you know they're out there). And never forget that every issue has two sides. . . .

In a lawsuit the first to speak seems right, until someone comes forward and cross-examines.
PROVERBS 18:17 NIV

Forgive me, Lord God, for the times I've jumped to bad conclusions. I don't like when others assume the worst about me, so please help me never to do that to others. I want to be kind and fair and always point other people to You.

85

Question: What do you call a man outstanding in his field?
Answer: A farmer.

Ha!

Yeah, that's a joke your great-great-grandparents probably told. It's an oldie, but it *is* clever, a way to poke fun at all the honors human beings hand out like candy at Halloween.

From the nationally televised Oscar, Grammy, and ESPY Awards all the way down to the blue ribbons at the tiniest county fair, people are eager to be recognized for their excellence. That's not a bad thing, as long as we're developing our God-given abilities to honor Him and are not just trying to impress (or possibly depress) other people.

But even if you're an Olympic-level athlete. . .even if you win the Nobel Peace Prize. . .even if you earn first place in a worldwide gaming competition. . .there's still something better to aim at.

You'll avoid a lot of regret in life when you

DO THIS

Excel at Trusting God

Those things that you're really good at all start somewhere. Sure, you have to work at your hurdling or drumming or woodworking or debate skills. . .but there's an even deeper source. That source, of course, is God. As the Israelites were entering their promised land of Canaan, Moses warned them about forgetting the Lord when they became successful. He warned them against ever thinking,

> " 'My power and the might of my hand has gotten me this wealth.' But you shall remember the LORD your God, for it is He who gives you power to get wealth." DEUTERONOMY 8:17–18 SKJV

Sooner or later, trusting in our own abilities will lead to disappointment. We all make mistakes, we sometimes get sick or injured, and ultimately each one of us will die. Not one human being has complete knowledge, goodness, or power. But God certainly does, and He's happy to apply all of His awesomeness to us when we simply trust Him.

> *You will keep him whose mind is steadfast on You in perfect peace because he trusts in You. Trust in the LORD forever, for everlasting strength is in the LORD JEHOVAH.* ISAIAH 26:3–4 SKJV

"PERFECT PEACE" SOUNDS GOOD, DOESN'T IT?

By all means, develop the skills and abilities God has given you. If you are good at something, aspire to be great at it. But never forget that the Lord gave you those gifts, and He wants you to use them for His glory. Like the biblical Hannah with her miracle baby, Samuel, give your gifts back to God. Trust Him with every part of your life—excel at that—and you'll never go wrong.

Those who trust in the LORD shall be as Mount Zion,
which cannot be removed but abides forever.
PSALM 125:1 SKJV

I trust You, Lord—but help me to trust You
more every day. Please help me to develop my
gifts to serve others and glorify You.

86 Brian couldn't believe it. He'd been fired!

If you asked him, Brian would say he worked harder than all his colleagues. He cared more about the finished product than anyone in the organization. He'd produced five years of exemplary work, but his boss was too stupid to see it.

But if you asked Brian's boss and coworkers, they'd say he got bogged down in the details, turning in every project late. He tattled on others who did things differently than he did. Then he chose to fight his supervisor rather than do what he was told.

More than a decade later, Brian hated the company and everyone in it. But his anger was only hurting *him*.

At times, we'll all think we've been wronged. But hanging on to offenses, stewing in our disappointments, only leads to regret. The solution?

DON'T DO THIS

Hold Grudges

Sadly, by hating his former coworkers, Brian had made himself crazy—without hurting them at all. Have you heard the saying "Cut off your nose to spite your face"? It seems a Latin version of the phrase goes back to the 1200s—proving people have been overreacting to their own hurt for a loooong time.

In Jesus' day, when John the Baptist criticized King Herod for marrying his brother's wife, Herodias was furious.

> *Herodias nursed a grudge against John and wanted to kill him. But she was not able to, because Herod feared John and protected him, knowing him to be a righteous and holy man.* Mark 6:19–20 NIV

Maybe you know that when Herod's birthday rolled around, Herodias' daughter danced for him and his guests. The king was so pleased that he offered the girl up to half his realm. She consulted with her mother, who demanded John's head on a serving tray. (*Gross.*) A dutiful daughter, the girl told Herod, who was compelled to honor his word. Herodias' grudge led to murder and—if she never dealt with her sins—serious justice from God.

The Old Testament hero Joseph had every reason to resent the older brothers who'd sold him into slavery—and, after his miraculous rise to power in Egypt, to crush them like bugs when he had the chance:

> *When Joseph's brothers saw that their father was dead, they said, "What if Joseph holds a grudge against us and pays us back for all the wrongs we did to him?"* GENESIS 50:15 NIV

READ THE WHOLE FASCINATING STORY IN GENESIS 37, 39–50.

But Joseph didn't hold a grudge—in fact, he assured the brothers that he would care for them and their families. This is the way everyone who follows God should think and act.

Trust God for justice and let go of grudges. Don't make yourself crazy.

Do not repay anyone evil for evil. Be careful to do what is right in the eyes of everyone.
ROMANS 12:17 NIV

Lord, You didn't hold a grudge against me because of my sin. May I never hold grudges against those who hurt me.

87 Does your school produce a yearbook? Do students still write messages in each other's copies? Once upon a time, at least, a popular sentiment was "I'll never forget you!"

But you know what? Over the course of years and decades, some of those people probably did forget their fellow students who at one time were very important to them. That's the nature of adult life—you get into a career, start a family, and take on a mortgage and other mind-consuming responsibilities, and certain details get pushed to the darkest corners of your brain. It takes some real coaxing to bring them back: "Oh yeah! Now I remember Jimmy. . . ."

Sadly, in the busyness of life, even God can get shuffled off to our mental storage spaces. Obviously, that's not a good situation. On your road to a no-regrets life,

DON'T DO THIS
Forget God

We can't blame modern society for the human tendency to forget God. More than three thousand years ago, Moses warned the ancient Israelites of that as they entered the promised land of Canaan:

> *"The Lord your God will soon bring you into the land he swore to give you when he made a vow to your ancestors Abraham, Isaac, and Jacob. It is a land with large, prosperous cities that you did not build. The houses will be richly stocked with goods you did not produce. You will draw water from cisterns you did not dig, and you will eat from vineyards and olive trees you did not plant. When you have eaten your fill in this land, be careful not to forget the Lord, who rescued you from slavery in the land of Egypt."* DEUTERONOMY 6:10–12 NLT

PROSPERITY IS A GIFT FROM GOD—AND OFTEN A CHALLENGE TO OUR FAITH.

We enjoy God's blessings every day. But because He's invisible to us, it's easy to focus on the world He created more than God Himself. We like our cars and our gaming systems and our sporting events and our girlfriends. . .and over time those things can nudge God further toward the edge of our consciousness. In the book of Ecclesiastes, Solomon waved a big red warning flag:

> *Don't let the excitement of youth cause you to forget your Creator. Honor him in your youth before you grow old and say, "Life is not pleasant anymore."* ECCLESIASTES 12:1 NLT

This is a great time to set good patterns for your life—to develop habits of Bible reading, prayer, Christian fellowship, and service that keep God front and center in your mind. Use the energy and enthusiasm of your teen years to good purpose. You'll never regret centering your entire life on the Lord.

> *O God, you are my God. . . . I lie awake thinking of you, meditating on you through the night.*
> PSALM 63:1, 6 NLT

Lord, please direct my thoughts to You each and every day. I don't ever want to forget You.

88 Overtime games automatically add drama to sports. While the hometown fans will always enjoy a blowout victory, those contests close enough to demand extra periods are much more exciting.

Most NBA fans hadn't even been born when the league's overtime record—six extra sessions—was set back in 1951. The Indianapolis Olympics edged the Rochester Royals 75–73 in that game.

Over in baseball, where the proper terminology is "extra innings," the American League's Chicago White Sox defeated the Milwaukee Brewers 7–6 in a 25-inning game that stretched over two days in 1984.

And then there's tennis, where a first-round Wimbledon match in 2010 went more than eleven hours over three days. American John Isner defeated Frenchman Nicolas Mahut 6–4, 3–6, 6–7, 7–6, 70–68.

No, that's not a typo. At that time, players had to win the fifth set by two games no matter how long it took. . .in this case, *138* games before the match was settled.

We can learn a lot from sports, and here's a great lesson:

DO THIS
Push through Hardships

We all like to win, no matter how exhausting the process. But the losers of such long contests can at least take satisfaction in their effort. Isn't it better to struggle and lose than to just give up when things get tough?

Though it's far more than a game, life demands a similar effort. You're not guaranteed success in anything you do—but you can be sure you'll fail if you quit.

As you do not know the path of the wind, or how the body is formed in a mother's womb, so you cannot understand the work of God, the Maker of all things. Sow your seed in the morning, and at evening let your hands not be idle, for you do not know which will succeed, whether this or that, or whether both will do equally well. ECCLESIASTES 11:5–6 NIV

Without a guarantee of success, hard work takes faith—faith in the God who calls you to obey Him now, with the promise of heaven to come. That's how Moses rolled:

By faith he left Egypt, not fearing the king's anger; he persevered because he saw him who is invisible. HEBREWS 11:27 NIV

MOSES' FAITH ALSO HELPED HIM AVOID THE "FLEETING PLEASURES OF SIN" (VERSE 25 NIV).

Whether you're playing a sport, struggling at school or work, trying to maintain a relationship, or even questioning your faith, you'll regret giving up too soon. Push through the hardships—and trust God to take care of the results.

"Surely the righteous still are rewarded; surely there is a God who judges the earth."
PSALM 58:11 NIV

Lord Jesus, sometimes I feel like quitting—but You pushed through the hardship for me. Strengthen me to do the same.

89 A man well into his fifties remembers a TV movie from his childhood. He couldn't tell you the film's title or who starred in it. But he'll never forget "that scene."

In the movie, set in the 1800s, a young boy had nursed a wounded crow back to health. Unable to fly, the bird became the boy's constant companion. One day, some local troublemakers came around, and the leader began throwing rocks at the crow. Laughing, the other boys joined in—and the bird's keeper, wanting to fit in, started laughing and throwing rocks too. Soon, the crow lay dead in the dust.

Okay, it's the guy writing this devotional who remembers that movie—and it still makes him cringe. That sad scene offers a powerful warning to all of us: never blindly go along with the crowd. Put another way,

DON'T DO THIS
Follow What's Popular

Not everything the crowd does is harmful—sometimes it's just silly, like ugly fashions and hairstyles. (Yeah, we're looking at you, 1970s and '80s.) But because human beings are selfish, sinful creatures, much of what the crowd does is awful. You know what happened after Jesus was arrested, right? It was "popular" to demand the freedom of a murderer and send Jesus to His death.

> *The chief priests and the elders persuaded the crowd to ask for Barabbas and to have Jesus executed. "Which of the two do you want me to release to you?" asked the governor. "Barabbas," they answered. "What shall I do, then, with Jesus who is called the Messiah?" Pilate asked. They all answered, "Crucify him!"* MATTHEW 27:20–22 NIV

The word *popular* comes from Latin, and simply indicates "of the people." The problem with "popular" is that "the people" are often stupid and wrong. Satan has lied to people since the beginning (John 8:44), and far too often we've swallowed his nonsense. When enough people join in, it's not only crows that get hurt.

Jewish leaders liked to stir up crowds against the apostle Paul. Once, in Corinth, they took him before the Roman governor Gallio:

> *Just as Paul was about to speak, Gallio said to them, "If you Jews were making a complaint about some misdemeanor or serious crime, it would be reasonable for me to listen to you. But since it involves questions about words and names and your own law—settle the matter yourselves. I will not be a judge of such things." So he drove them off. Then the crowd there turned on Sosthenes the synagogue leader and beat him.* ACTS 18:14–17 NIV

OF COURSE, PAUL GOT BEATEN TOO—REGULARLY.

Following crowds is dumb—because their ideas are rarely God's. Never jeopardize your faith, with all the regret that accompanies that, by doing the "popular" thing.

Wisdom will save you from the ways of wicked men.
PROVERBS 2:12 NIV

Give me strength, Lord, to stand apart from the crowd.

90 Many homes have a certain wall or doorframe that's all marked up—but not by kids. It's from Mom and Dad keeping a record of Junior's physical development. Each year, the parents make him stand in the same spot in the house, where they then use a pen or pencil to note his increasing height.

Physical growth is the normal expectation for kids. You start as a helpless little baby. You gain size (and attitude) as you become a toddler. Your stature increases as you enter school and work up through the ranks. Now, as a teenager, you're actually nearing the end of your physical growth. Whether you top out at five feet or seven, make sure you also

DO THIS

Grow Up Spiritually

You never had to think about physical growth. As long as you were eating, playing, and sleeping, God made your body develop. Of course, it's God who provides your spiritual life too, through your faith in Jesus—but you have an important responsibility to participate in its growth.

We've already seen the apostle Peter's command to "make every effort to add to your faith goodness; and to goodness, knowledge; and to knowledge, self-control; and to self-control, perseverance; and to perseverance, godliness; and to godliness, mutual affection; and to mutual affection, love" (2 Peter 1:5–7 NIV). As you "make every effort," you are joining with God in your own spiritual growth. And then,

> *if you possess these qualities in increasing measure, they will keep you from being ineffective and unproductive in your knowledge of our Lord Jesus Christ.* 2 PETER 1:8 NIV

Childhood should be a wonderful time. The whole world is new and exciting. Fun and play are big elements of your day. But that time doesn't last forever. As your body develops and you become a man, your spirit should follow suit. Here's how the apostle Paul described the process:

> *When I was a child, I talked like a child, I thought like a child, I reasoned like a child. When I became a man, I put the ways of childhood behind me.* 1 CORINTHIANS 13:11 NIV

NOTICE THE ACTIVE VERB PAUL USES: *"I PUT* THE WAYS OF CHILDHOOD BEHIND ME."

None of this means you can't have fun—the Christian life is supposed to be full of joy (see Nehemiah 8:10; Psalm 51:12; 2 Corinthians 8:2; and Galatians 5:22, among many other scriptures). But life is serious. You'll regret delaying your Christian manhood by holding on to childish things. It's time to grow up spiritually.

Brothers and sisters, stop thinking like children. In regard to evil be infants, but in your thinking be adults.
1 CORINTHIANS 14:20 NIV

Childhood was fun, Lord—but help me now to grow up into the Christian man You want me to be. May I work with You to become serious and mature while holding on to a sense of wonder and joy.

91

Many aspects of God are completely beyond our human understanding. A lot of people get frustrated by that—but it's actually a good thing. If we could fully understand God, He wouldn't be God. You'd be either equal or superior to Him, which is a crazy thing to think. (And you wouldn't want responsibility for the whole universe anyway.)

Because God is all-knowing and all-powerful, His desires will be accomplished. We won't always see or grasp His working, but in the end, God's will—as Jesus prayed in the Lord's Prayer—will be done, in His own time and way.

We'll be happier and more fulfilled as we obey what God clearly reveals in His Word, trusting Him with the details He hasn't made plain. Do what you know is right, and

DON'T DO THIS

Be an "In Spite of" Christian

Sometimes God has to work around His people. If we're not living as we should, He will accomplish His plan *in spite of* rather than *because of* us. Here is Paul describing God's end run around certain preachers who envied the apostle's ministry:

> It's true that some are preaching out of jealousy and rivalry. But others preach about Christ with pure motives. They preach because they love me, for they know I have been appointed to defend the Good News. Those others do not have pure motives as they preach about Christ. They preach with selfish ambition, not sincerely, intending to make my chains more painful to me. But that doesn't matter. Whether their motives are false or genuine, the message about Christ is being preached either way, so I rejoice. PHILIPPIANS 1:15–18 NLT

Were Paul's rivals true Christians? Maybe, maybe not—but God could use them for His good purposes either way. Only the truehearted, pure followers of Jesus, though, would enjoy God's blessing.

The famous story of Esther shows how God will get His way whether we obey Him or not. The words of Mordecai indicate that God *wants* but doesn't *need* us in His plans:

> "If you keep quiet at a time like this, deliverance and relief for the Jews will arise from some other place, but you and your relatives will die. Who knows if perhaps you were made queen for just such a time as this?" ESTHER 4:14 NLT

AND *YOU* WERE PUT HERE, NOW, FOR GOD'S PURPOSES TOO.

Don't create regret in your life by avoiding or resisting God's commands. He'll get what He wants in spite of you—why not advance His plan because of you?

> *"You will know that I am the LORD, O people of Israel, when I have honored my name by treating you mercifully in spite of your wickedness. I, the Sovereign LORD, have spoken!"*
> EZEKIEL 20:44 NLT

Father God, give me the wisdom and courage to do what You want, every time. Help me to play an enthusiastic part in what You're doing in the world.

92 You're walking through the neighborhood and see a fast-food bag lying by the curb. Do you (a) ignore it, (b) think, *Why doesn't someone do something about that?,* or (c) pick it up and throw it away?

You step into the kitchen and notice that someone has tracked dirt across the floor. Do you (a) ignore it, (b) shout, "Mom! There's dirt on the floor!" or (c) grab the broom and dustpan and sweep it up?

You borrowed your parents' car to take some friends to a game. Returning home late at night, you notice the gas gauge is hugging E. Do you (a) ignore it, (b) think, *Dad will fuel up on the way to work tomorrow,* or (c) circle back to the gas station and fill the tank?

Perhaps you noticed the pattern here: Our first choice is often to ignore something that needs attention. Or we tend to off-load the responsibility. Or we could—the best choice—just jump in and fix things.

Here's a rule that will make the world a little better place—and in this crazy world, every little bit helps:

DO THIS

Leave Things Better Than You Found Them

Can you imagine if everyone was watching out for simple ways to improve their homes, their schools, their churches, their towns? And not just watching, but actually following through? Such "good deeds" don't save your soul, of course, but they do make your world just a bit nicer. And whether anyone else ever notices what you're doing, God certainly does.

Do not forget to do good and to share, for God is well pleased with such sacrifices. HEBREWS 13:16 SKJV

It doesn't take much effort at all to leave things better than you found them. You just have to keep your eyes open to opportunities and then commit to doing what needs to be done. Put your brother's cereal box back in the cupboard? Check. Fill the dog's water dish? Check. Wipe the smudge off the mirror? Check. Pull that weed in the mulch bed? Check.

When you do good deeds around unbelievers, you might even get the chance to tell them *why*—and then you can give the credit to God, who constantly works to improve human lives.

> "Let your light so shine before men, that they may see your good works and glorify your Father who is in heaven." MATTHEW 5:16 SKJV

YOU ARE THE "LIGHT OF THE WORLD," YOU KNOW (VERSE 14 SKJV).

Never miss a chance to do something good, no matter how insignificant it may seem. Sometimes the little things carry more weight than you'd ever guess.

In all things showing yourself a pattern of good works.
TITUS 2:7 SKJV

*Give me the eyes to see opportunities for good works,
Lord—and then a voice to share Your truth with anyone
who asks. I want everyone to ultimately glorify You.*

93 Even a Hall of Famer starts out as a rookie—with some lessons to learn along the way.

Reggie Miller (Basketball Hall of Fame class of 2012) enjoyed a stellar career at UCLA and became a first-round pick in the 1987 NBA draft. He joined a league where Michael Jordan, in his third season, was redefining pro hoops.

In an exhibition game early in his first season, Miller's Indiana Pacers faced Jordan and the mighty Chicago Bulls. The rookie outplayed the superstar in the first half, scoring 10 points to Jordan's 4. Egged on by a teammate, Miller started jawing: "Oh, so you're the great Michael Jordan, huh? There's a new guy in town!"

MJ didn't say much in response. He just outscored the rookie 40–2 in the second half.

Sure, mouthing off to opponents is a long-standing tradition in sports. But you'll avoid regrets in life when you

DON'T DO THIS
Talk Trash

To his credit, Miller tells the story above with a laugh. But most of us won't reach his level of success—our big mouths will just embarrass us. And embarrassment = regret.

The Bible always talks truth, not trash. And here's what it says about the way we as Christians should use our words:

> But now you must also rid yourselves of all such things as these: anger, rage, malice, slander, and filthy language from your lips. Do not lie to each other, since you have taken off your old self with its practices and have put on the new self, which is being renewed in knowledge in the image of its Creator. COLOSSIANS 3:8–10 NIV

When the picky, irritable Pharisees attacked Jesus' disciples for eating without first washing their hands, Jesus taught that what goes *into* a person's mouth doesn't defile him—it's what comes *out* (Matthew 15:1–20). Along those same lines, the apostle Paul wrote that since our attitudes and words reflect on our Lord, they should all be good:

> But among you there must not be even a hint of sexual immorality, or of any kind of impurity, or of greed, because these are improper for God's holy people. Nor should there be obscenity, foolish talk or coarse joking, which are out of place, but rather thanksgiving. Ephesians 5:3–4 NIV

FOR MORE ON CHRISTIAN SPEECH, SEE JAMES 3:1-12.

Trash (or trashy) talk just doesn't suit followers of Jesus, the adopted sons of God the Father. Stop the snark and replace it with respect. Ditch the dirt and speak what's spiritual. You'll save yourself from regret and hopefully point others to the Lord who died for their sins.

Those who guard their lips preserve their lives, but those who speak rashly will come to ruin.

Proverbs 13:3 NIV

I need Your help, Lord, to control my mouth. Guide me into pure and respectful talk so others hear You through me.

94 These days, you hear a lot of people arguing that private property is somehow immoral and oppressive. (Though it's interesting to note how often those same people have nice homes and plenty of resources to travel around sharing their ideas.)

The Bible often talks of private property, describing people's houses and flocks and fields and money. The assumption seems to be that human beings can and should own things. God distributes stuff to people as He sees fit (see Ecclesiastes 5:18–19), and we have the opportunity and responsibility to develop what He's given us (see Proverbs 13:11).

Honestly building your private wealth honors God. Shortcuts and cheating do not. Here's an important rule to commit yourself to:

DON'T DO THIS
Steal—Anything

You probably already know this, but the Ten Commandments—God's most basic rules for humanity—forbid theft. Here's number eight of the Lord's Top Ten:

> *"You shall not steal."* EXODUS 20:15 NIV

That's a simple rule with a wide application—because there are all kinds of ways to steal. It's not just that you change your name to "Rob Banks," you know.

If you download copyrighted music, movies, or games without paying, that's a form of stealing. If you carry off supplies from your school or workplace, that's a form of stealing. If you just waste time on your job, that's a form of stealing too. If you say yes when God says no, there will be consequences. They may be bigger or smaller, sooner or later, but disobedience in any area of life leads to regrets.

Throughout its many pages, the Bible condemns stealing. But the apostle Paul adds a positive command to all the negative ones:

> *Anyone who has been stealing must steal no longer, but must work, doing something useful with their own hands, that they may have something to share with those in need.*
> EPHESIANS 4:28 NIV

PAUL ALSO TAUGHT, "THE ONE WHO IS UNWILLING TO
WORK SHALL NOT EAT" (2 THESSALONIANS 3:10 NIV).

Stealing is wrong because private property is God's idea. But the idea of private ownership never justifies greed and stinginess in His people. John Wesley, the eighteenth-century preacher whose teaching became known as Methodism, preached a sermon called "The Use of Money" with three main points: "Gain all you can," "Save all you can," and "Give all you can."

Just never steal anything. And if you have, why not make it right?

> *If you suffer, it should not be as a murderer or thief*
> *or any other kind of criminal, or even as a meddler.*
> *However, if you suffer as a Christian, do not be*
> *ashamed, but praise God that you bear that name.*
> 1 PETER 4:15–16 NIV

Lord, it's easy to want more without wanting to put in the work. If I'm ever tempted to steal, remind me that Your way is for me to develop the skills and resources You've given me.

95 There are few things in life worse than being lied to. That used car dripped oil all over your driveway after the salesman insisted it was fully reconditioned. . .the customer service rep promised your money would be refunded, but it never showed up in your bank account. . .Madison said she couldn't go out with you because of a family event, but you saw her sitting at the restaurant with another guy.

You know it hurts to be on the receiving end of a lie. So be very careful that you never inflict that pain on someone else. In this life, you'll avoid regret if you strive to

DO THIS

Be Honest

Truthfulness isn't the most popular thing in this world. If people think dishonesty will gain them an advantage, they'll gush lies like a volcano spewing lava. But the Christian guy should never let himself do that. Why? Because we serve a God of perfect honesty.

"God is not a man, so he does not lie." Numbers 23:19 NLT

"And he who is the Glory of Israel will not lie, nor will he change his mind, for he is not human that he should change his mind!" 1 Samuel 15:29 NLT

"All who invoke a blessing or take an oath will do so by the God of truth." Isaiah 65:16 NLT

This truth gives them confidence that they have eternal life, which God—who does not lie—promised them before the world began. Titus 1:2 NLT

> *Jesus replied. . ."I say only what I have heard from the one who sent me, and he is completely truthful."* JOHN 8:25–26 NLT

JESUS CALLS HIMSELF "THE TRUTH" (JOHN 14:6).

There are times when it's scary to tell the truth. We're tempted to lie when we've done something stupid—but whatever we did wrong is only magnified when the truth ultimately comes out. And it does.

Of course, there are also times when a so-called little white lie would seem to protect another person's feelings—but be very careful even of those. For example, if a girl is more interested in you than you are in her, don't give her kind but dishonest words that lead her on. The Bible's command is this: "Speak the truth in love" (Ephesians 4:15 NLT).

Sure, it's a cliché, but honesty is your best policy. Live your life wisely, speak the truth in love. . .and if you ever run into a dicey situation, just tell the truth and let God sort out the details. He's not going to honor a lie, you know.

Better to be poor and honest than to be dishonest and a fool.
PROVERBS 19:1 NLT

*Heavenly Father, please give me the wisdom
to live my life honorably and, when necessary,
the courage to speak truthfully. I want to be
honest like You—the first time, every time.*

96 In 1987, back when kids (maybe even your parents) were riding dinosaurs to school, the song "Material Magic" was airing on contemporary Christian radio stations. Singer-songwriter Wayne Watson described the stress—and the foolishness—of burning yourself out for money and stuff. "Funny thing is," he sang, "it can all blow away."

However successful you become, your physical things are destined to disappear. To avoid regrets, in this world and the next,

DON'T DO THIS

Be Materialistic

"Material Magic" ultimately led listeners to the only guaranteed savings plan—in the Bank of Heaven. That's what Jesus taught, so you know it's true: "Don't store up treasures here on earth, where moths eat them and rust destroys them, and where thieves break in and steal. Store your treasures in heaven, where moths and rust cannot destroy, and thieves do not break in and steal. Wherever your treasure is, there the desires of your heart will also be" (Matthew 6:19–21 NLT).

The apostle Paul followed that plan. In his second letter to Christians at Corinth, he said the hardships and shortages he experienced while serving God really didn't matter to him:

> *We own nothing, and yet we have everything.* 2 CORINTHIANS 6:10 NLT

How is that possible? As a committed follower of Jesus, Paul was assured of an eternity full of blessing and pleasure (see Psalm 16:11), no matter how much or little he had on earth. The reward was coming.

Paul was a unique case—he led a much tougher life than his fellow Christians, many of whom faced deprivation themselves. Most of us will always have enough food and clothing, and at least a decent place to live. With our basic needs supplied, let's ask God to make us content. . .how cool would it be to simply wave off more stuff?

> "What were all the flocks and herds I met as I came?" Esau asked. Jacob replied, "They are a gift, my lord, to ensure your friendship." "My brother, I have plenty," Esau answered. "Keep what you have for yourself." GENESIS 33:8–9 NLT

JACOB WAS TRYING TO MAKE UP FOR STEALING ESAU'S BIRTHRIGHT (GENESIS 25:29-34).

Yes, we need money and physical things to live in this world. But most of us need a lot less than we think we do. And there are always people around us with even fewer resources. Though it may seem crazy, work harder at sharing stuff than getting it. God will take care of you as you take care of others.

Don't let the "material magic" work its spell on you.

> **"You should remember the words of the Lord Jesus:**
> **'It is more blessed to give than to receive.' "**
> ACTS 20:35 NLT

Lord, I'm a material guy in a material world—but I need to live by Your Spirit. Remind me that You'll always provide for my needs, so I can be free to pursue more important things.

97 For an author, a book like this is tricky. The challenge is to create something that teen guys will find interesting and helpful but not preachy or judgmental. Be assured of this: Paul Kent isn't looking down from some ivory tower. He's had plenty of regrets and wishes he would have made better choices.

All of us will do the wrong thing at one time or another. We'll be selfish and foolish. We'll be rude and careless. We'll commit sins large and small, by accident and entirely on purpose. Our wrongdoing should never be waved off as unimportant, but it also should never derail us permanently.

If you've done things you regret, take heart. Look up. Breathe. Whatever you do,

DON'T DO THIS

Think You Can't Be Forgiven

God knows you're going to fail sometimes. He knew it before you were born. He knew it before He created the universe. But He also had a plan to deal with it.

That plan was the death of Jesus on the cross. One perfect man took the punishment for the sins of billions of imperfect people. When you believe in Jesus by faith, God washes your sins away and saves your soul. And then, after you've been "born again," He keeps washing your sins away—day after day—when you simply admit the things you did wrong.

> *If we tell Him our sins, He is faithful and we can depend on Him to forgive us of our sins. He will make our lives clean from all sin.* 1 JOHN 1:9 NLV

"TELL HIM OUR SINS" = "CONFESS" IN OTHER BIBLE TRANSLATIONS

Since we live after the life, death, and resurrection of Jesus, we have a clearer view of how God's grace works. But even BC, before Christ, in Old Testament times, God was showing mercy to His people. . .who did some really atrocious things. The prophet Isaiah shared the good news that God was always ready to forgive:

Let the sinful turn from his way, and the one who does not know God turn from his thoughts. Let him turn to the Lord, and He will have loving-pity on him. Let him turn to our God, for He will for sure forgive all his sins. ISAIAH 55:7 NLV

Consider this: One of the very worst kings of Judah encouraged his people to worship idols—and even sacrificed his own son to a false god. But "when Manasseh was in trouble, he prayed to the Lord his God, and put away his pride before the God of his fathers. When he prayed to Him, God heard his prayer and listened to him" (2 Chronicles 33:12–13 NLV).

If God could forgive Manasseh, He'll forgive you. Just ask.

"Those who have sorrow are happy,
because they will be comforted."
MATTHEW 5:4 NLV

I don't want to live with regret, Lord.
Please forgive my sins and give me Your joy.

98 You've probably heard the saying "A friend in need is a friend indeed." That's easier to understand if you fill in some unspoken words: "A friend in *your time of* need is a friend indeed."

It's not a Bible verse—not even from the legendary book of Hezekiah—but it's certainly true. Friends will be there for you, in any kind of trouble. They show up quickly with a listening ear, a can of gasoline, a fistful of dollars, or a fresh pizza. They come over, in person, to meet whatever need you have—physical, financial, emotional, or spiritual.

Don't overlook the incredible importance of human relationship. For a no-regrets life,

DO THIS

Make Real Friends and Be a Real Friend

You may have dozens, perhaps hundreds of "friends" on social media or your gaming network. But likes and follows don't mean much when your car breaks down late at night. And SmellyDog0128, who's such an amazing partner in the shoot-'em-up games, won't hang with you after your girl has said adios. He probably lives in Outer Mongolia.

These are the times you want a real, live, hometown friend, someone who enjoys your company as much as you enjoy his. . .someone who will drop everything to actually be with you when you need him.

Two are better than one, because they have a good reward for their labor. For if they fall, the one will lift up his companion, but woe to him who is alone when he falls, for he does not have another to help him up. ECCLESIASTES 4:9–10 SKJV

THAT'S A CLASSIC!

The Bible was written long before social media changed the whole concept of "friending." But its principles of friendship are just as timely as ever:

> *A man who has friends must show himself friendly.* Proverbs 18:24 skjv
>
> *Iron sharpens iron; so a man sharpens the countenance of his friend.* Proverbs 27:17 skjv
>
> *A friend loves at all times.* Proverbs 17:17 skjv

You want a friend who really cares about you. But you should also aspire to *be* that person for someone else. True friendship is clearly a two-way street, but also a "three-stranded cord," in the words of Ecclesiastes 4:12 (skjv). That third member of the group? God.

Even if you don't "need" friends now, you will. Get away from the screen and make some real-life connections. That's a trade you'll never regret.

And it came to pass, when he had finished speaking to Saul, that the soul of Jonathan was knit to the soul of David, and Jonathan loved him like his own soul.
1 Samuel 18:1 skjv

Lord, guide me into the kind of friendship that helps us and honors You.

99 Imagine you're driving through a major city. You're on a multilane superhighway with thousands of other drivers in cars, SUVs, delivery vans, and semitrucks. They're all doing around eighty-five miles an hour, zipping in and out of lanes, trying to get to their destination yesterday.

This is no time to lose focus.

To stay safe, you need to stay sharp. You have to keep up with the other drivers and make sure you don't wander out of your lane. You don't dare take your foot off the gas or your eyes off the road. That could be disastrous.

Now imagine *life* is that crazy, multilane highway. You're flying along with dangers on every side. To stay safe, you need to stay sharp. Whatever you do,

DON'T DO THIS
Coast Mentally

God made human beings to work (see His command to Adam in Genesis 1:28). And not just physically—we need to exercise our minds as much as our muscles. When we coast mentally, bad things happen. . .and bad things lead to regret. Here's the prelude to the incredible collapse of King David, known as a man after God's own heart:

> In the spring of the year, when kings normally go out to war, David sent Joab and the Israelite army to fight the Ammonites. . . . However, David stayed behind in Jerusalem. Late one afternoon, after his midday rest, David got out of bed and was walking on the roof of the palace. As he looked out over the city, he noticed a woman of unusual beauty taking a bath. 2 SAMUEL 11:1–2 NLT

In case you don't know how the story ends, it's not pretty: David sends a servant to bring the woman to him, he sleeps with her, and then he orders her husband killed.

This is the man who was handpicked by God to be king of Israel. This is the man who wrote nearly half of the psalms in your Bible. This is the man whose family line produced Jesus Christ, the Savior of the world. When David got careless, when he coasted mentally, he lived to regret it.

Never set your mind on idle. Your life must be all about the conscious mental pursuit of goodness.

> *Clothe yourself with the presence of the Lord Jesus Christ. And don't let yourself think about ways to indulge your evil desires.* ROMANS 13:14 NLT

"LET YOURSELF THINK" = COASTING

Is it easy to always be on guard mentally? No—it's work. It takes a commitment to read God's Word and pray and deny yourself often. . .sometimes even to get up and go somewhere else for a while, until the temptation to coast passes. But this is a commitment you'll never regret.

I stay awake through the night, thinking about your promise.
PSALM 119:148 NLT

Please keep me sharp, Lord—for Your sake and mine.

100 The publisher of this devotional once created a book of Christian quotations. Interesting, inspiring quotes were collected and grouped by topic. The editor was proud of the finished work. . .but ten years later, when using the book as a reference for another project, he got depressed.

Why? Because so many of the people quoted—pastors, writers, musicians, and other important people—had crashed and burned morally. Within a decade, they had "fallen into sin". . .or at least their private sins had become public.

It's disappointing to see people who know better destroying their lives and ministries. But let's be honest—*we* know better, don't we? So let's make sure we never fail like that. Here's an important guideline:

DO THIS

Start Thinking of Your End

Yeah, you're still young. You probably have fifty, sixty, maybe even seventy years yet to live. It might seem morbid and weird to think about the end of life.

But we're all getting older, heading toward that common human destiny: death. And whether you live twenty years or a hundred, you'll want to end well. For Christians, that means staying faithful to Jesus all through life, like the apostle Paul did:

> *I have fought the good fight, I have finished the race, I have kept the faith.* 2 Timothy 4:7 NIV

What exactly does Paul mean? Practically speaking, how do you fight a good fight in life? How do you finish this race and keep the faith?

As is often the case, other parts of the Bible explain. In the Gospels, Jesus Himself tells how to finish well:

> *"As for everyone who comes to me and hears my words and puts them into practice, I will show you what they are like. They are like a man building a house, who dug down deep and laid the foundation on rock. When a flood came, the torrent struck that house but could not shake it, because it was well built."* Luke 6:47–48 NIV

YOUR ASSIGNMENT: HEAR JESUS' WORDS AND PUT THEM INTO PRACTICE.

This life is short. Men in their eighties and nineties will tell you that time flies. But our short life is too long to live with the regret of moral failure.

Just to be clear: We'll all sin from time to time, and God is happy to forgive any sin we confess. But never allow sin to become "acceptable" in your mind—then you're just asking for trouble.

It's never too soon to start thinking of your end. Make decisions every day that keep you on track, and God will make sure you succeed.

Blessed is the one who perseveres under trial because, having stood the test, that person will receive the crown of life that the Lord has promised to those who love him.

JAMES 1:12 NIV

"Show me, Lord, my life's end and the number of my days; let me know how fleeting my life is" (Psalm 39:4 NIV).